I0066661

It's Banking Jim, But Not As We Know It

Creating tomorrow's bank by identifying the most critical strategic changes and trends in banking today

Book 3 of The Complete Banker series

By Chris Skinner

The
**Complete
Banker**

First published 2010 by Balatro Limited, 98 Westbury Lane, Buckhursthill, IG9 5PW, UK

ISBN 978-1-907720-08-6

Edited and produced by Searching Finance Ltd, 8 Whitehall Road, London W7 2JE, UK. Tel: +44 (0) 7885 441682; email: enquiries@searchingfinance. co.uk; web: www.searchingfinance.co.uk

Editor: Ann Tierney

Typeset by: Deirdré Gyenes

It's Banking Jim, But Not As We Know It

Creating tomorrow's bank by identifying the most critical strategic changes and trends in banking today

Book 3 of The Complete Banker series

By Chris Skinner

The
**Complete
Banker**

About Chris Skinner

Chris has been providing independent, expert commentary on the key developments in banking for over a decade in his role as Chief Executive of Balatro and Chairman of the Financial Services Club. In particular, he has been writing for various media, such as the Banker Magazine, since 2004 and is a key commentator on banking for prime time news channels including the BBC, Sky and Bloomberg. Prior to creating his independent entities, Chris had key roles at management and board levels covering insurance, retail and investment banking across a range of consulting and technology firms.

Chris Skinner has worked worldwide delivering advice, keynote speeches, presentations and workshops to many banks and vendors worldwide, including Accenture, American Express, ANZ, Bank of America, Bank of Baroda, Cisco, Hewlett Packard, Liberty Bank, Lloyds TSB, McKinsey, Merrill Lynch, Microsoft, National Australia Bank, Nationwide Building Society, NCR, TATA, the National Bank of Kuwait, the Union Bank of the Philippines, Wachovia Bank, Washington Mutual, and many others.

About the Financial Services Club

The Financial Services Club is a unique service aimed at senior executives and decision makers from banks, insurance companies, technology firms, consultancies ... in fact, any firm that is interested in understanding and planning for the future operating environment for the financial services markets.

The Financial Services Club bridges the gap between today and tomorrow. It allows you to network with hundreds of professionals all sharing a common interest in the future of the industry. The Club hosts over 50 events a year, in a number of different European countries, with keynote speakers and luminaries from the industry airing their views on the future of financial services. Our illustrious speaker list is targeted to cover all aspects of the industry from practitioners to legislators to futurists.

For more information, go to http://www.fsclub.co.uk

Contents

It's Banking Jim, But Not As We Know It

Chapter 3 Banking technology

Chapter 4 The great channel debate

Chapter 5 The mobile future of banking

Chapter 6 Changing customer relationships

It's Banking Jim, But Not As We Know It

Chapter 7 Marketing in the new media age

Chapter 8 Long term thinking

Preface

I spend my life in the future. Not literally, although it feels that way. I've worked the future for over 15 years now, since co-creating the Knowledge Lab in NCR, the Global Future Forum in Unisys and Shaping Tomorrow in my independent life.

But I'm not a futurist.

You see, my interest in the future is purely because it's the one thing none of us knows for certain. The future is uncertain. However, if you could identify the most critical things likely to occur in the future today, then you could capitalise commercially upon the opportunities presented. And that's where my interest lies.

It makes me a commercial strategist.

Note the subtle difference: futurists are just interested in anything remotely in the future; commercial strategists are interested in anything in the future that might help them make money.

So that's what this book is all about: what are the most critical things that will occur in banking tomorrow that, if you invest in them today, mean that you can make your fortune.

A simple enough premise, and one that I hold to be very true.

For example, I predicted the overwhelming power of mobile internet finance in 2003. By 2009, most people had got the message.

I predicted that the complexity of derivatives combined with increasingly automated quant analytics would result in systemic risks that would make those markets implode in 2005. In 2008, the credit crisis hit and in 2010 the "flash crash" implosion on Wall Street.

These are all areas where commercial strategists can have success.

I'm not always right, of course. For example, I predicted that 90% of bank branches would be of no use to traditional branch-based banks in 2005.

Mind you, there's still time.

So, if you want to work out how to the most successful bank you can be during the next decade, then this is the book for you.

Meantime, if you want to become a complete banker, then keep adding our small works of observations about the industry to your knowledge by buying some of the other books about banking in the Complete Banker series.

Have fun and enjoy the read,

Chris

PS: The articles herein have been selected from white papers, presentations and other research I have undertaken, and from my regular Financial Services Club blog postings at http://www.thefinanser.com; for more information on the Financial Services Club, go to http://www.fsclub.co.uk

Chapter 1 Facing the future: bank strategy in uncertain times

Introduction

As mentioned, the future is the one thing that's uncertain which is why it's worth tracking. The way you track the future is through futures trends, extrapolation, using forces for change models, such as PESTLE, and more. One of the most successful methods of facing the future is to use scenario modelling, where you look for all extremes of change and, by doing so, can handle any or all of them. I was lucky enough to work with the World Economic Forum on such scenarios in the build-up to Davos a few years ago, and it makes for interesting analysis. Mind you, it didn't forecast the financial crisis, so you might wonder how useful these things are. The answer is, on their own, not very, but if you combine all of these methods and your own intellect, potentially something very powerful. Here are a few ideas that came up in my own mind over the past few years.

Scenarios for the future of banking (2009)

Yesterday, I gave a presentation on the future of banking. This is because I specialise in the future of banking. When I say that I specialise in the future of banking, most people ask: "Is there one?" An awful lot of people think there is no future in banking, but they are wrong. Of course there is a future in banking ... it's just that no one knows what it is or what it looks like right now. So here's my way to clarify it.

First, use Michael Porter's forces of change. Michael Porter's forces are based upon the key drivers of impact upon a company, which are Political, Economic, Social and Technological or PEST for short**. What's the PEST in banking, apart from regulators and politicians? Reasonably obvious.

1 : Facing the future: bank strategy in uncertain times

Politically, lawmakers are desperately trying to come up with ways and means to get some stability back into the system to restore confidence, control and credibility.

Economically, the seizure in lending and liquidity is driving down economies worldwide. Apart from major concerns related to protectionism and retrenchment, economists are trying to figure out whether we are facing normality, stagflation, deflation, or something worse. (*ed: Reformation, Revolution, Armageddon?*)

Society, meanwhile, has completely lost confidence and trust in bankers and policymakers. Therefore, they are postponing spending, with savings levels rising for the first time in years in many of the 'borrowing' economies.

Technology continues to develop at a pace meanwhile, with everything completely transparent. Nothing can be hidden anymore. As a result, new models of access to financial services are arising, such as Zopa, Prosper, Wonga, SmartyPig, the new MTFs and clearing systems for trading, the Barter Network, complementary currencies.

It's Banking Jim, But Not As We Know It

• **Political**	• **Economic**
– Loss of control and credibility	– Debt exposures
– Massive debt burdens and tax implications	– Dependency on SWFs
– Nationalisation through osmosis	– Cross-border friction
– Co-ordinated global response	– Protectionism
– New regulatory regime	– Stagflation and deflation
	• **Technological**
	– Transparency of media
• **Social**	– Anyone can be a news channel
– Housing market implosion	– Social media and social networking
– Negative equity	– Facebook and Twitter
– Loss of savings and pensions	– Saas, Widgets and access
– Trust erosion	– Alternatives to Banks
– Zero confidence in politicians, financiers or media	

+44 790 586 2270 Chris Skinner@fsclub.co.uk

All in all, the outlook is one where politicians have lost control, the economy is spiralling downwards, society doesn't trust anyone and technology is allowing them to find out why and get around the system.

What does this mean for the future of the industry?

It leads to four scenarios, all of which have a semblance of truth.

The four scenarios are based upon two key axes: the banking model is either fundamentally broken or fixable on one, and banks are the only providers of finance or there are alternatives on the other.

The alternatives to banks are not necessarily non-banks by the way, but could be new banks. In this context, just as MiFID created a whole raft of innovative new ventures in the trading arena – Chi-X, Turquoise, NASDAQ OMX, BATS Europe,

1 : Facing the future: bank strategy in uncertain times

Equiduct, Quote MTF, Burgundy, EMCF, EuroCCP – the theory would be that new regulations to cure the banking crisis creates new ventures for finance as an alternative to traditional ones.

Looking at these axes of extremes leads to four scenarios for the future of banking:

The Financial Services Club

Scenarios for the Future

Return to the old ways
Banks get a severe reprimand and heavy government oversight for a few years but, over time, old ways creep back in with new ways to arbitrage, hedge, trade and invest. The exposures and losses of this crisis unlikely to repeat for decades, but another crisis will happen within the next decade.

Fixable

Industry restructuring
The opening of the banking model to new players creates new competition and new models of banking. Governments determine to encourage transparency and openness, and use regulations to allow 'trusted' institutions to enter the markets. These would include retailers and telco's.

Banks only ← → **Alternatives to banks**

Nationalisation
If banks are the only providers of financial services and the model of banking is fundamentally broken, then governments have to take over the system for the foreseeable future. The result will be lethargic and tentative financial markets, which feed government budgets with protectionism. A lose-lose for all.

Broken

Wild West
Technology allows new players in finance from Europe's MTF to new providers of finance such as Zopa, to create a revolution in the industry. Governments are powerless to manage these changes, because the markets are turbo-charged by consumer and corporate connections to technology.

© Chris Skinner. All rights reserved.   +44 790 586 2270 Chris Skinner@fsclub.co.uk

1) Banking is fixed and banks are the only players. This leads to a continuance of the old model of financial servicing with traditional providers still in a position of strength and liquidity is focused upon the traditional key markets and organisations. Result: we survive this crisis but experience another one in five to ten years ... hopefully, not as bad as this one.

It's Banking Jim, But Not As We Know It

2) Banking is fixed and alternatives to banks are created. The regulators and politicians encourage new regulations and supervisory frameworks that lead to new providers of service, such as the new CCP for OTC Derivatives. These new providers may be an amalgam of existing players and/or new industry consortia, and it drives a flight to safety by encouraging the largest and most secure firms to act cohesively to create confidence. Result: we survive this crisis and the weakest fail, whilst new confidence comes intoo the system through a comprehensive industry restructuring.

3) Banking is broken and alternatives to banks take over. This is a wild west of new finance where regulators and banks are avoided due to either (a) declining business; (b) being unable to take on board business that's offered; or (c) not being offered the business in the first place. Result: consumers and corporates are forced to use new models of finance and banks fail as new players take over. This also has the outcome of a financial system that is fragmented and uncontrollable.

4) Banking is broken and banks are the only players. This is the worst case scenario where banks that don't want to be nationalised are nationalised by governments that don't want to nationalise them. Banks become puppets of Minsters of Finance and are seriously debilitated in the face of an onslaught of regulations and red tape. Result: everyone loses and no-one wins.

Right now, the world sits in a hybrid of all four quadrants, with the most likely outcome being an amalgam of all four. I just hope that the dominant scenario is the industry restructuring (top right) though, as the lower two quadrants are scary and the top left is probably unacceptable.

It will be interesting to see the results over the next year or two.

** Some refer to this as PESTLE and include Legal and Environmental forces for change, as well as Political, Economic, Societal and Technological.

Technology strategy is the bank strategy (2008)

In banks today, technology strategy is the essence of business strategy.

In capital markets, where algorithmic trading analytics can make the difference between success and failure, technology is critical to competitiveness. If you cannot compete with another bank's new derivatives capabilities, which are driven by technical excellence, you might as well give up the ghost. If you lose a millisecond of speed in the investment markets, you are dead. That is why low latency is at the core of capital markets today and technology strategy is at the core of latency.

This is why an exchange said to me, "If it takes more than 500 milliseconds to process then it is of no value because it is out-of-date". Technology strategy is the core focal point for the exchange.

This is why an investment firm said to me, "We moved servers to Moscow because it takes 60 milliseconds to route a trade from London to Tokyo via Moscow compared to 240 milliseconds if we process the trade via New York". Technology strategy is the core focal point for the bank.

This is why investment firms are co-locating their servers within exchanges. It is also why we are seeing market blips occurring on a regular basis, because markets move in real-time.

In capital markets, technology strategy is at the core of business strategy.

This is also true in commercial banking. For the commercial banker, faster payments are all about real-time payments. SEPA is all about replacements of technology infrastructures. And the supply chain for the corporate client is all about straight through processing.

In corporations, especially manufacturers, you can now transport goods as cheaply from Guangzhou to Grantham as you

It's Banking Jim, But Not As We Know It

can from Gillingham to Grantham. How come? Because mass container shipping has made the transport of skyscraper-sized boats full of goods a reality. Hence, the cost of shipping a box of shoes from Guangzhou is now as cheap as shipping a factory full of shoes.

This is due to standards. And the standard is a container box.

In the financial support of that supply chain, there are no standards. Therefore, banks are scrambling to work with SWIFT on SCORE, MA-CUGs and TSUs; with ISO on ISO20022; and with TWIST on implementing e-invoicing standards, bank services billing standards, and other standardised processes for straight-through processing.

All of this is about making the bank easy to do business with, which means plug-and-play connectivity, real-time reporting, and value-adding information services for the corporate client. In other words, technology strategy is at the core of business strategy.

This is also true in retail banking. Many of us believe that retail banking is all about branches.

Rubbish. Branches are just sales stores today, as transaction services have moved out of the branch to the ATM and the internet. In other words, retail bank customers serve themselves online through automated systems, and in real time.

This self-service culture is going to be even more pervasive as retail banks offer more services across electronic mobile channels, as well as introducing new payments channels using chip technologies. New payment channels are critical to the war on paper: cash and cheques. Yet, paper is the only reason customers go into branches these days, purely because they cannot process paper, cash and cheques, electronically so they cannot serve themselves.

The result is that retail banks purely have electronic connections with their customers. In other words, technology strategy is at the core of business strategy.

So, technology is at the core of the strategy deployed in retail, commercial and investment banking. It is the foundation of banking in the 21st century. You cannot reduce and downgrade the import of getting technology right or wrong.

Now the challenge.

Bearing in mind that technology is fundamental to client relationships, is obsolete the day you buy it, is disruptive and changing at a speed that is hard to keep up with, then the bank has to place technology as the cornerstone of their business strategy. It is the most important aspect of the bank's business strategy.

Put it in the context of a bank being like a human body. The brain of the bank is the executive management, who set strategy. The heart of the bank is the people, the organisation structure, the front line staff. The skeleton of the bank is the buildings, bricks and mortar. And technology is the nerves, veins, muscles, tissues and blood for the bank. It keeps the bank body connected.

The brain is the IQ of the bank, with some being more intelligent than others. The heart sets the culture of the bank, and it is hard to copy a culture. The skeleton is rarely broken but has to be on occasion, as branches are moved and new markets opened.

But if the nerves, blood and veins of the bank are clogged, blocked or hardened, then the bank will die. It is not the brain that stops thinking; it is the blood to the brain. It is not the heart that stops beating; it is the blood flowing through the heart. Bones do not disappear; it is the blood and tissue.

A bank's blood flow is its technology, as that's the only thing that connects all of the disparate pieces of the bank together.

This is why technology strategy is the bank strategy in today's world.

Battleground 2010: Sharks versus Gorillas (2010)

After West Side Story, the Sharks got over the Jets and are now targeting the Gorillas.

Actually, nothing to do with music or film – we're talking banks.

Back in the 1950s you had large banks (Sharks) being run around by small banks (Jets) who were nimbler and quicker ... so the large banks acquired them and the Sharks became Gorillas. Now we have large banks that are strong (Sharks) running rings around large banks that are weak (Gorillas), whilst the small banks (Jets) still run circles around both of them.

What am I talking about? Bank's competitive strategies for the teens (2010s).

Today, we have three camps of banks:

◆ Those that are major universal / regional banks with strong balance sheets;

◆ Those that are major universal / regional banks with weak balance sheets; and

◆ Smaller, independent or mutual banks with a major customer focus.

It is clear who falls into which camp as the first camp are those cited in the major surveys as being expansion banks like Santander, JPMorgan, HSBC, ICBI; the second camp is the bail-out banks like Bank of America, Citibank, RBS, Lloyds, Fortis; and the third are the credit unions, mutuals, building societies and sparkassens.

What is intriguing today is the strategies that each camp will take.

For example, if I were a Shark then I would look to acquire strength by buying weakened banks and by offering 50 basis point discounts on my savings and loans products. No-brainer, and exactly what Santander has been doing in buying cheap banks assets that are positive to the balance sheet – deposit holders, branches, savers and prime rate customers from Alliance & Leicester and Bradford & Bingley.

The thing is, this puts a strain on the conversion process for integrating merged systems and infrastructures, as demonstrated by some of the poor reviews of Abbey which may ripple over onto A&L and B&B. Equally, it places spotlight firmly onto the account opening, client onboarding and customer acquisition processes, as these banks firmly focus upon gaining market share.

The result is that the Sharks will be investing big time in M&A platforms that are open and easy to develop and evolve, whilst shining internal energies on re-engineering the client onboarding processes to make them as simple and effective as possible.

Which leaves the back-end customer retention processes exposed, which is where the Gorillas will be making their investment. A Gorilla has little opportunity to grow new customer share, as they cannot offer the rate churns that the Sharks will be putting into play. As a result, their focus has to be upon customer retention and share of wallet. Cross-sell ratio, product margin, incentives to invest more will all be priority for a Gorilla as they aim to strengthen balance sheets. Loans and leverage? Maybe not. Give those to a Shark or even to a Jet.

The nimble Jets are the credit unions and mutuals of this world. They grow and gain business by "not being banks" and they focus on customer needs because their customers are not customers. They are members. And the Jets are not profit-focused, but member-focused. As a result, many of them will do whatever it takes for the customer, and naturally offer very competitive interest rates and strong member (customer) retention processes that promote advocacy and loyalty.

So there we have it.

The Gorillas are snuffling about slowly, whilst the Sharks cut a dash. The Jets are diving upon both and sometimes winning, but it's no big deal as the Gorillas and Sharks are still dominating the scene. All of them have a singular focus, however, upon customer and customer processes. They all are trying to excel at the customer process of onboarding and retention. Their focus just varies depending upon their theme for competitive activity.

Fragmenting the banking structure (2009)

Most banks have evolved from days of branches and large offices, to banks with multiple channels of distribution and extensive technology backbones. The issue banks have with this structure is that the technology backbone is broken.

This is well illustrated by a comment from one payments manager who said to me that he gets his highest rating for performance if he changes nothing. This is because the complex beast of transaction processing is best left alone. If it ain't broken, don't try to fix it. Leave it well alone.

But this just isn't good enough anymore. Not only does it mean that banks are intransigent to change, but they will also be outsmarted by new players.

For example, it's already seven years since Europe determined to introduce the Payments Services Directive and the Single Euro Payments Area, and we still have no end date in mind, nor do we have any idea how to get our customers to migrate to these instruments.

Many say it will be 2018 or after before we get to a fully-integrated Eurozone. That would make it a 16-year change program.

Similarly, most banks will admit that there are so many councils created to provide governance over the change of these systems, that you can only move at the speed of the slowest player

... that is why change is so slow in the backbone infrastructures of this industry.

But it won't be slow for the new entrants: the payments institutions. It wasn't slow for PayPal, which has rapidly become one of the largest payments processors by volume of transactions, and yet they are not even 10 years old.

What PayPal achieved, and other payments institutions will do the same, is not just to build innovation on the old, out-of-date, legacy backbones ... but to completely rethink the payments process as a layer of innovation above the backbone. This will happen more and more with other payments institutions.

Where this leads is that banks need to fragment themselves.

Break the bank into pieces.

Each piece should represent a piece of functionality, a process, a capability.

And for each piece of functionality, a process, a capability, the bank should ask hard questions: are we good at this? Should we be doing this? Could we provide this service to other banks? What would it mean if we did? How much do our customers value this? Would they pay for it?

Without this hard analysis, banks will stagnate in the sandpits of historical approaches, where legacy builds upon legacy, and the bank tries to serve all customers across all channels in a bank managed way. Doing the above results in average and will never be exceptional.

Instead, banks should focus upon who they are trying to reach and serve, and in what way. They should then look to see which areas of this service they can deliver exceptionally and, where it is average or below average, either improve it or junk it.

This means that the old way of banking, where the bank would deliver the entire infrastructure, product and service in a vertically integrated package, is no more.

Today, for banks to compete, they must focus upon where they have strengths, and outsource the rest to the best provider of the services they need to offer around their core competencies.

Equally, a bank must stop believing that they can serve all of the people all of the time. That is the reason banks have expensive legacy overheads because they are trying to keep the old products alive for the old customers, whilst trying to innovate services at the other end for the new customers.

The result of a bank believing they have to do everything internally end-to-end and serve all customer demands from legacy customer channels and instruments to new ones, is failure.

Banks must rationalise to categorically reach and serve the customers they want to reach and service the best, and internally restructure to process and manage only the parts of the customers' processes they are strong at delivering internally whilst outsourcing the rest to the best.

Simples!

Real-time risks and opportunities (2009)

What are the risks for the next year or two?

First, we are still in the middle of what I call the internet, or www, recession. There are still foreign exchange and trade issues between China, Europe and the USA, and doubts over sovereign debt defaults in key countries such as Dubai, Greece and Ireland. In addition, we still have a UK AAA-rating risk of downgrade, as do other countries, and all of this will make 2010's economic recovery a challenge, although not as hard as this year has been.

Second, we are seeing a major contraction in debt amongst businesses and consumers. This means that those who can pay-off debt are doing so, leaving those who want to borrow or increase debt being those who are increasingly viewed as being higher risk because of their need. This will potentially result in a 'debt squeeze'. The debt squeeze is where banks are left with the people who want lending being those they can't lend to, whilst those they can lend to are the customers who don't want it and have paid it back.

Third, there are still risks, especially liquidity risks, that will require banks to seek further diversification of risk by either entering new markets or, more likely, pulling out of all markets where risks are less quantified. This could still lead therefore to national protectionism, where a bank actively seeks to focus on known home territories, whilst selling off or shutting down any more recent and therefore less known expansionism.

Fourth, there are issues of corporate governance as mentioned by John McFall.

Fifth, there are the nerves created by the change of leadership of the management of the internal markets of Europe, from the City-friendly Irishman Charlie McCreevy to the unknown but pro-French minister Michael Barnier.

Finally, there is a challenge with technology, in that there is fast cycle change in technologies in the front office areas of retail banking (mobile) and trading rooms (high frequency trading) versus very slow change in back office infrastructures (SEPA is now seven years old and interoperability in clearing and settlement is still to happen). This dual carriageway of slow-lane back office and fast-lane front office technologies is going to crash somewhere in the middle, unless something is done to align the two better.

On the opportunities for the next year or two.

First, things are cheap. If you are a bank with liquidity, then you can pick up a bargain these days. This is no better demonstrated than JPMorgan with Bear Stearns and Washington Mutual, or by Santander with Alliance & Leicester and Bradford & Bingley. If you have capital, then today is a low hanging fruit picking season.

It's Banking Jim, But Not As We Know It

There are also opportunities for those who can innovate. With so many firms focused upon operational excellence and internal management issues, firms that have clearly unblinkered and unfettered capabilities to compete can begin to decimate.

Some of this opportunity is being created by deregulations that have been years in the making. For example, non-bank payments institutions in Europe could sweep up a lot of activity now that they can be registered for processing under the Payments Services Directive. MiFID is still allowing change and competition for the MTFs, with Chi-X and BATS taking a lump or two out of those markets.

Most important of all, of course, are the ability for new banks to enter weak markets. This is why the UK has flurry of new banks, from Virgin and Tesco to Metro and the Post Office.

Therefore, strong, well-capitalised, financial institutions and non-banks can start to cherry pick much of the banking market profitability if they want, leaving the incumbents with the festering gristle.

So, all in all, here's the message.

For most banks, 2010 will be a return to basics and a focus upon getting the most efficiency and effectiveness out of operations. Operational excellence will still be the key management competency. This was the focus for 2009, but the 'back to basics' approach will be even more resonating and loud.

Real-time reporting will be critical from all angles, especially from a risk reporting viewpoint. The FSA has been pushing for real-time liquidity reporting, and it would not surprise me if a move towards real-time clearing and settlement becomes a focus on the table. That's the focus of trading exchanges, such as Eurex or the Russian exchanges, and real-time is also becoming a focus in the retail world as the march of faster payments progresses. So real-time everything will be key.

1 : Facing the future: bank strategy in uncertain times

Finally, intimate customer knowledge and using the tools for strong customer analysis with data mining tools will be high on the agenda. As bankers, many are looking for more cross-sell opportunities and you only get those if you have customer intimacy. This is key.

(...)

Why is it that innovations are created by non-banks? (2008)

At SIBOS 2004 in Atlanta, Heidi Miller of JP Morgan delivered a keynote address that is still discussed to this day. This is because she asked four critical questions of us:

◆   Why do we make things so complicated for our clients?

◆   How can we help our customers become more efficient and productive, when our own back offices are so expensive, fragmented, outdated and 'non-interoperable?

◆   If we can send a secure message to any company over the internet, why should we pay SWIFT to do it for us?

◆   If we truly aspire to be leaders in the payments and securities industries, why is it that so many innovations in this business are pioneered by non-banks?

Now, I am not intending to review the progress we have made in these areas four years later, but I am going to pick up on one of these questions: innovation. Innovation is the focal point for so many discussions with banks right now.

Banks are suddenly discussing innovation everywhere, and trying to work out whether it is a process, a science, a quirk or a revolution. For example, if you review the annual reports of the Top 10 American banks, the use of the word 'innovation' has doubled in frequency since 2001 to an average 6.5 appearances per report these days. Equally, almost every bank has a Head of Innovation today, tasked with finding out how to make the bank a 'thought leader', 'differentiated form the pack' and 'clearly on the leading-edge'.

These heads of innovation try to stir up the executive with new ideas: a passion for fashion, a neck for tech and a dash for cash. I know, let's offer all of our customers a credit card that can also be an iPod. No, give everyone a contactless keychain. Or maybe get the bank launched into Second Life and become a virtual bank. All of these ideas are worthy and worth exploring, no matter how mad you think they are, as without experimentation and trial, banks will stagnate. And yet, how many serious innovations are there out there, and how many have really come from within the industry?

This was a question posed recently by my friend, John Chaplin. John is known for his work in the cards arena on SEPA and advisory work with First Data, and he recently decided to ask a global panel of payments experts, including myself, about our views on innovation.

His definition of innovation is that it involves more than just turning a new concept into a commercial success, more than just technology and more than just an evolution. It is taking an idea and transforming that idea into a commercial business model that is successful, determined, can be implemented and proves itself to be worthy.

The experts came from nine different countries including Denmark, Dubai, Finland, France, Malta, Norway, Slovakia, UK and USA; and all experts have lived or worked in multiple countries. Previous and current employers include Co-operative Retail, Deloittes, DNB, First Data, Honeywell Bull, IBM, Link, MasterCard, Moneybox, NCR, Nordea, Tietoenator, Tower Group and Visa.

Here's what he discovered.

Who innovates first?

We all stated that new entrants and technology providers are the innovators in payments, not banks, processors or payment schemes. Why? Because "existing major players have invested too much in either shared or individual infrastructures to want to make major changes and, in many cases where the existing business model creates good profitability, why take the risk to change things?"

Aha! So Heidi Miller's premise holds true with the global industry expert panel.

Why are banks innovating or trying to innovate anyway?

Mainly for revenue generation and new client acquisition. These are clear drivers, although they are closely followed by cost reduction as a focus. However, reinforcing the former point, several experts believe that new entrants innovate first because they see the opportunity to create a profitable business by either undercutting the incumbent or creating new opportunities to generate revenues by offering a different service into the market.

Which region is the most innovative?

The panel felt that Asia is the most innovative payments region, followed closely by America. Europe and other regions lag. This is because Asia (and Africa to be honest) are creating radical changes through mobile technologies, remittances and other services, especially, China, Japan and Korea. That does not mean that the USA is lagging, but the America's focus more on internet services, with PayPal mentioned often as a major innovator.

Europe is viewed as being too fragmented and held back by the baggage of legacies to be innovative. For example, one expert's comment was: "Sorry about that mediocre score for Western

It's Banking Jim, But Not As We Know It

Europe. SEPA's great, but ten years in the making seems more like evolution than innovation."

Hmmmm ... a little over the top if you ask me, but might be right. In fact, the panel went as far as to say that SEPA will reduce innovation. This is because, in the short term, innovation will suffer as technology investments are focused upon the modernisation of legacy infrastructures. However, the panel did at least admit that, in the longer term, SEPA should create an environment in which innovation will increase.

Where will innovation start: low value or high value payments?

On this point, all of the panel were clear that low value payments are where innovation is focused. This is partly because you can experiment more here but it is more down to the fact that, with higher value payments, the risks of innovation are higher and you do not want to jeopardise high value payments through innovation therefore. It is also because lower value payments are perceived to be more inefficient and therefore a clear target for innovation.

The survey asked several other questions, such as:

◆ How will lower interchange impact innovation?

◆ Where will innovation be targeted?

◆ Is there one innovation which would particularly benefit the payments industry?

But the one I thought was interesting to note is whether the panel could name any firms who would lead innovation on payments. Here's who they came up with: Amazon, Apple, Equens, First Data, Google, MasterCard, PayPal, SIA, Tencent QQ and Visa.

Anyway, going back to Heidi Miller's speech, it is interesting to see how insightful her words were, in light of the survey mentioned above. Here's what she actually said:

> "Wouldn't you think that banks should be facilitating payments transactions for e-Bay? We have the customer relationships. We have the accounts. We have the clearing and settlement systems. In fact, Pay Pal transactions ride on the very same systems we banks have spent billions of dollars building. And yet the banks lost the deal, despite our natural advantages ... Kudos to PayPal for their creative innovation. And to Checkfree in electronic bill payment. And to ADP and Paychex in Payroll Processing. And to First Data in merchant processing. And to Radianz in IP network connectivity. Shame on us. We repeatedly allow ourselves to be disintermediated. By the time we have barely gotten ourselves organized, nimble new competitors have staked out their superior claims."

So maybe not that much has changed in four years?

Banks aren't charities, so why do we treat them that way? (2010)

Banks aren't charities and yet the non-stop bleating about bonuses and interest rates would make you think they should be run as though they were not-for-profits. But banks aren't not-for-profit; they are proprietary firms with stock listings. They are there to make money, not to exist for the public good.

So what's gone wrong? Unfortunately, during the past two years, the line between public and private has blurred, as evidenced by the Royal Bank of Scotland and Northern Rock, or by Citi and Bank of America in the US, or HVB and Commerzbank in Germany, or UBS in Switzerland or ...

The fact that these banks were bailed out by their respective governments, albeit temporarily in most instances, has blurred the media and public's view of what they are there for. The media and general masses now think they own the banks or, at least, have some skin in their game. And sure enough, in the case of RBS and Lloyds, the UK taxpayer does have some skin in the game: 84% and 43% respectively.

But that doesn't mean the taxpayer runs the bank or that they exist for the public good.

In the case of RBS and Lloyds, they actually now exist in a shadowland where they are competing with openly aggressive trading firms like Goldman Sachs and JP Morgan, whilst having to conform with the requirements of the Treasury and UKFI.

This causes this schizophrenia between being openly competitive versus being humbly contrite.

What a pain. But look at the bottom line: these banks are still private firms with stock listings who have to serve their shareholder first. That's why they are paying bonuses, restricting lending, avoiding risk and being competitive. Or that's their thinking.

This is why we find it so hard to determine the right approach to bonuses and remuneration.

But take this a step further and we now have the journalistic and taxpaying community believing that they should somehow determine the interest rate setting policy and fees of the bank. For example, over the weekend, the BBC got itself into a tizz over credit card interest rates. The question posed is why, when the Bank of England's interest rates are at their lowest levels ever, are banks charging the highest rates ever on credit card balances?

The answer is simple. The credit card portfolio runs as its own division with its own P&L. Today, more folks are defaulting than ever before. As the risks are greater and bad debts increasing, the interest rate has to rise accordingly.

The media and public then say: but you're paying out all these hefty bonuses, what about us? Decrease the bonuses so that you can reduce our credit interest rates.

C'mon now and be serious.

The investment bank doesn't subsidise the card portfolio. They are separately run businesses with their own P&L and both are tasked with making a profit, so both run their book as competitively and profitably as possible.

That's why Barclays announced an increase in overdraft fees on deposit accounts just two days after saying that BarCap's bankers would get an average bonus and pay package of just under £200,000 each for the 23,000 staff in that division. You see, the latter achieved their annual objectives and targets, so that's why they deserve it.

And all of this is in a competitive battlefield where anyone can walk – both staff and customers.

But it ain't that easy.

First, Barclays are justified in their actions because they never dipped into the taxpayer's pocket, unlike RBS and Lloyds. Therefore, are RBS and Lloyds justified in providing bonus packages in the same way as Barclays? If they are privately held, shareholder-owned competitive banks, yes; if they are semi-nationalised, taxpayer-funded state-run banks ...

In addition, the divisional components of the bank may be independently structured by their P&L but that argument doesn't hold water when the bank would have gone under in the case of RBS, Citi and others, thanks to the failings of that very part of the bank that is now sharing the spoils amongst their staff at the customer's and taxpayer's expense.

It is this blurring of the lines between a nationalised business that should operate in the public's interest versus the privatised industry that operates in the shareholders' interest that is causing all of the media and general debate today, whether it is about

It's Banking Jim, But Not As We Know It

bonuses, remuneration, profits, fees, interest rates or any other aspect of banking.

This half-hearted, schizophrenic shadow of an industry that doesn't know whether it's coming or going, and has no idea how to regulate itself or be regulated, needs a strong hand to steer it to an objective and vision for future operation.

That vision appears to be one of an independent industry, run under free market principles with shareholder focus as its central tenet.

If you don't like it ... lump it.

Chapter 2 The new economics of banking

Introduction

Looking towards the future of banking, there are many rapid-fire changes taking place, although you would not notice them if you were a banker or a customer of a bank. This is because banks don't do any rapid-fire change. They just follow change once it is proven to be required. However, the new reality of the new generation of mobile internet based banks may change this as the new economics of banking become a reality. What are the new economics of banking? Why, that banking should be free, of course. After all, news, entertainment and most other digitised products are available for nothing, so why not banking?

Why banking will be free (Part 1) (2009)

Some people cannot understand why I blog everyday and so frequently, especially as it's free. They actually think I should charge something for this stuff!

Sure, it would be nice, but I learned a long time ago that being free is far more effective than charging for everything. In particular, I spent some time with Kevin Kelly, senior maverick and launch editor of *Wired* magazine, a decade ago and he told me that everything would become free.

I thought he was nuts at the time, but how wrong was I?

Kevin has 12 lessons about how to think about the internet, and they were difficult to absorb as, bearing in mind this was back in 1997, he was far too ahead of his time.

Anyways, I went back to these lessons and re-read them today. The reason being is due to the amazing way the internet is changing our world, and that it occurred to me, just like music and newspapers, banking will soon cost nothing. Loans and payments will be provided for free.

I guess, to explain this one, we need to understand Kevin's lessons, which he put into an article entitled: "New rules for the new economy", back in *Wired* in 1997.

In summary, the lessons were:

1) The Law of Connection: Embrace dumb power
With everything having an inbuilt computer chip connected to a network, start thinking about how to use those inbuilt chips.

2) The Law of Plentitude: More gives more
In the networked economy, there's loads of everything and little of nothing. There is no scarcity, because it costs nothing to churn out more. This means the more you give for nothing, the more you get of everything.

3) The Law of Exponential Value: Success is non-linear
Because everything is connected, small changes can explode into global and seismic movements overnight. Just look at Facebook and Twitter if you want to see this one in action.

4) The Law of Tipping Points: Significance precedes momentum
The tipping point – the point at which something goes from being a micromarket to the stage of critical mass where everyone has got one, like the iPod – occurs at a much faster rate and a much lower point of mass in the network economy.

5) The Law of Increasing Returns: Make virtuous circles
The more people in the network, the more value of the network. As a result, every additional member increases value exponentially.

6) The Law of Inverse Pricing: Anticipate the cheap
It used to be that quality improved with higher prices in the industrial age; in the internet age, quality improves with lower prices over time. The law of price:quality has flipped.

7) The Law of Generosity: Follow the free
Because value increases with abundance, and the cost of production is virtually nothing to create more copies, flood the market with copies of your product for free because the more who have

It's Banking Jim, But Not As We Know It

it, the more valuable it becomes and the easier it becomes to sell product adjuncts.

8) The Law of the Allegiance: Feed the web first

Networks have no clear centre or boundaries and therefore no clear organisation. You cannot feed a network top-down, so feed it first as the only 'inside' now is whether you're on or off the network.

9) The Law of Devolution: Let go at the top

Everything is dispensable. A network market domination can be replaced just as quickly by a new one. Just look at Friends Reunited, displaced by Facebook. Or AOL replaced by broadband general accessibility. Sell when you have reached the peak, not after.

10) The Law of Displacement: The net wins

The question: "how big will internet commerce be?" is irrelevant as everything will be on the net.

11) The Law of Churn: Seek sustainable disequilibrium

Instead of leaving businesses, people will just continually morph businesses and improve them in a never-ending rebirth process through the net.

12) The Law of Inefficiencies: Don't solve problems

Create ideas and put them out there unformed, as the net will finish them. You don't need to solve problems, just start ideas. Linux is a great example.

I don't intend to discuss them all, but the one that really got me back then was #7: follow the free.

Follow the free? What, give everything away for nothing? You must be mad.

Unfortunately, that's what everyone thought about Kevin back then. What Kevin was really getting at, is that the more you build a following, the more valuable you become. The more valuable you become, the more you can charge a premium for stuff.

Today, this is far more obvious but, back in 1997, Google, Facebook, Linux and all the other good things of today's web were not around. We were back in the AOL, Microsoft Windows '95 and fax era.

Today, it is obvious that if you have a million or more regular daily users, you can sell advertising and sell other nice 'add-ons' to those users. But remember that these are not locked-in users. They are more like fans.

Fans of Google, Facebook and Linux could dump these products overnight for a better version, just as Yahoo! search fans, Friends Reunited fans and Microsoft's fans have done (only a little bit in the last case).

So, this brings us back to where I started. I blog for free because I enjoy it and one day it may bring other forms of reward.

A bit like newspapers. I get free newspapers these days, but they are paid for by the advertising in the paper and propped up by website services linked to the paper. These days, the *Guardian, Telegraph, Sun* and *Evening Standard* get far more web traffic than any newspaper revenues or sales ... and their web traffic is provided for free because each click generate advertising revenues.

This is what the newspaper industry misunderstood to start with, but now they get it big time.

It is also what the music industry misunderstood and is now just starting to get. These days, you don't sign music artists to write songs and sell records, you sign them to write songs and give them away for nothing so that people will follow their website, buy the t-shirts, come to the gigs and download the odd track. This is why entertainment firms sign their artists up for 360-degree contracts these days – all the music sales and the rest – rather than for a recording contract.

Which bring me around to banking.

I talk a lot a lot about banks and social networks, Web 2.0 and all, but one thing I didn't say is that banking will cost nothing.

Just like newspapers, blogs, music and even books and live streaming rock concerts, banking will be free. My payments will be processed for nothing. My loans will be charged at zero margin, as will my savings.

PayPal, Zopa and SmartyPig are already dabbling with these models of new business for banking, but it is still early days.

So here's my vision of the new world order.

Banks offer me all of their administrative and transactional services for no charge. There is no charge on being in the red and yet I still get good rates when I'm in the black.

So how does the bank make money? First, by having millions of us in their community

Second, by partnering with firms which advertise and provide services to my millions of financial community members.

Third, by selling that community ancillary products and services – hats, t-shirts, nice leather binders and folders, umbrellas (if you don't get this one, just look at ING Direct).

Fourth, by providing me and the corporate customer with some real value, such as aggregation services, lifestyle financing advice, real-time risk management, identification of missing tricks and more.

The latter points would be things like alerts that say: "do you know your pension will only pay you half of what you earn? Top up your pension premiums now ... you can afford it", and showing me graphically and visually why it makes sense. The same could be true for investments, loans and other products.

For the corporate customer, it might be real-time portfolio and cash management positions for treasurers to improve allocation of resources; real-time analysis of market and credit movements to ensure minimisation of exposures; real-time tracking of products and finances through global windows to financial services and supply chain systems; and more.

The fact is that it is the value the bank adds in the fourth tier that really locks me in, because the bank can then get under my skin and into my brain.

This will be the new bank model and the new bank order post this crisis will weed out those who get the follow the free model and provide real value, versus those transactional banks that are just processors.

The latter bunch will be more link internet connections – cheap, cheerful commodities. The former group will be the banking Facebooks and Googles of the future.

I can't wait to join them.

BaaS: Banking as a Service (2009)

Banking as a Service (BaaS) is the new version of banking using the Software as a Service (SaaS) business model.

You're probably all familiar with SaaS – it's basically paying for applications as you use them, rather than buying them – and a great example is Salesforce.com. I would also contend that Google's getting to be the biggest SaaS through its email, word processing and other apps. These services used to cost you a fortune, but are now free or near enough.

That's where banking is going.

Banking becomes plug and play apps you stitch together to suit your business or lifestyle.

There's no logical reason why banking shouldn't be delivered as SaaS. In fact, it is already for some folks. For example, here's my banking with no bank involved:

It's Banking Jim, But Not As We Know It

The Financial Services Club

Banking as a Service

Skinner's Bank

Digital Wealth Card

◆ BANKFREEDOM™

z•pa

APR
£6,000
36 months

Rate: 8.7% for
lowest risk
borrowers

12.8% for highest
risk lenders

PayPal

©Chris Skinner +44 790 586 2270 chris.skinner@fsclub.co.uk

Using prepaid cards, I can load up and get a MasterCard and just keep topping up without ever using a bank. Just look at Bank Freedom's website description:

"Enjoy the convenience of a prepaid card that acts just like a regular credit card, with a Prepaid MasterCard® Card. Prepaid MasterCard cards are paid in advance and are easily reloadable, which makes it a great alternative to carrying cash. Offering you the same safety and security as a regular MasterCard card, a Prepaid MasterCard card allows you to make purchases or cash withdrawals at an ATM. Prepaid cards are a safe and reliable alternative to traveler's cheques. When using a Prepaid MasterCard card, purchases are automatically deducted directly from your card balance, which can be easily topped up."

Equally, using Digital Wealth cards, I can get prepaid cards without limits. The card can be loaded using wire transfers, Western Union, MoneyGram, E-Gold, e-Bullion, Pecunix, WebMoney, and Liberty Reserve, and allows $3,000 per day or

$90,000 per month to be withdrawn through 1.3 million ATMs worldwide.

Alternatively, I could use PayPal, Google Checkout, Bill-Me Later and other services for payments, although some of these need a bank account to open an account with them.

For my savings and investments, the best deal comes from sites like Zopa. Today's borrowing and lending rates on Zopa are excellent: 12.8% for the highest risks on my lending, which I can insure, versus 8.7% interest for the lowest risk borrowers. The UK's best savings rates right now are 3.55% for example, and I can get a loan for 8.9% from Alliance & Leicester, but most are charging 11.9% or higher.

All in all, it would be an interesting experiment to load up on these services and try living on prepaid cards, revolving balances on PayPal and savings and borrowing through Zopa, just to see how long you could survive off the banking network.

I might try it some day.

I even think corporates could do this, and some do by running their own bank internally. However, I'm thinking that, using BaaS, corporates would build a full financial service using providers such as First Data, the Barter Network, PayPal, Google Checkout and related services. I'm not sure they should do this, but it could be interesting to see how far you could push the boat.

What I'm really getting at here is that the old model of banking, where everything is packaged together around a deposit account with a cheque book, is bust.

That's why some banks are starting to white-label and break apart their traditional services so that corporates can just buy-in the bits they like and want. That might be a SWIFT Gateway here, internet payment services there, international money transfers here, cheque processing there ... all bits of banking, all prices and packaged to plug and play as a service.

It's Banking Jim, But Not As We Know It

For corporates and consumers, there will also be niche operators who use BaaS to offer new banking models as integrators. These integrators bring the pieces together – Mint and Wesabe are already not far off the mark – and provide them in a far more competitively prices model than traditional banks.

This is the future bank, and old banks will need to reconsider their services to compete with this zero margin model.

Final thought: Banking as a Service. Think about it. Banking ... as a Service.

Now that would be nice, wouldn't it?

Note: I avoided any mention of sheep.

Banking on a widget (2009)

BaaS is based upon Software as a Service, a method of taking complex applications and offering them as web services where you pay for what you use. BaaS is just applying the same concept to banking services.

Widgets are parts of applications offered as simple pick up and drop code on the network. Programmers have developed these so that anyone can just lift them into their web pages if they want to, and have the right permissions.

So what's the point?

The point is that BaaS allows banks to be decoupled into their constituent components and offered as widget-based functionality through the net. It's radical but obvious, and applies to all aspects of retail, wholesale, investment and payments functionality.

I specifically outlined some basic attributes of BaaS earlier, but my thoughts have come on a little since as shown here. For example, I've taken Ken Harvey's (CTSO, HSBC) comments about banking on the network, and used them to illustrate how BaaS has real power.

Ken makes the point that he can launch in any country and it is just the physical bits that cost: the buildings, offices, branches and advertising. All the IT is free, because HSBC build it once and then deploy globally through the network so that it can be used by thousands of staff and customers in almost 200 countries.

Note: one program build for thousands of users in hundreds of countries.

Once you have network enabled components, you can add any branch, product or even country onto the network for zero extra cost.

That's the power of BaaS.

BaaS means that any module, component or function of a bank can be application packaged and network enabled as a banking widget. The balance statement widget; the payments transaction widget; the loan application widget; and so on.

BBVA realise this, as demonstrated by their *Tu Cuentas* service, but most banks do not get it which means that new players, such as PayPal, Zopa, SmartyPig, Wonga and more, could step in and deploy widgets for loans, savings and payments.

Using such widgets within BaaS allows a bank or new entrant to gain customers with no extra work as, once built and deployed, there is no extra cost for more on the network.

Ten years ago, running the Financial Services Club would have cost around $800k in mailing, printing and telephone costs. Of this, about $150k would be the cost of physical meetings. Today, the only costs are for those physical meetings.

The digital network – blog, emailing, website operation etc – is near enough free from a costing perspective, apart for our own time and effort, as Typepad, Facebook and more create zero cost operations.

This is the challenge for banks. A decade ago, 70% of costs in materials that are now free would have been a big barrier to entry. Today, they are not.

That's what Ken Harvey (HSBC) makes clear. HSBC can enter any country with a mortgage, credit card or new branches, and the only costs are above-the-line marketing (that could even be free on YouTube) and physical infrastructures such as buildings. The rest is on the network.

And it's not limited to retail banking either, as the new European equities exchanges are demonstrating. Chi-X, Turquoise, BATS Trading, NASDAQ OMX and more are all launching radical new trading systems using leading-edge technologies at a tenth or more of the cost of the traditional exchanges.

They also have a tenth or less of the staff and overall, this is why these new trading venues can charge 10 basis points per side to clear and execute trades in under 2 milliseconds compared to seven times the cost and many times the time taken by the incumbents.

Any area of financial services you want to point to, I could show you new entrants and innovative incumbents changing the model using the concepts of BaaS and the network.

Combining these thoughts, BaaS with banking widgets delivers:

1) The ability to grow without any additional costs – just add more traffic on the network;
2) Componetise the bank into widgets that can be picked up and dropped by staff and customers as they feel;
3) The opportunity for staff and customers to create banking homepages that are completely personalised to them;
4) The integration of banking functionality from one bank with others, in a completely flexible aggregated manner;
5) Future-proofing for the semantic relational networking of the next generation web; and
6) Totally flexible, totally comprehensive, low cost, high tailorability for every part of the banking organisation.

That's pretty powerful and compelling, as the bottom line is that anyone could now launch a widget for a banking app and make it available anywhere.

The question will then be: which widgets do you trust, which raises the old nugget of banking regulation, licences and other barriers to entry.

Some things are much slower to change!

Free: the new economics of banking (2009)

This posting comes around because I was thinking about banking on the network and whether banks really will give away banking for free. So here's how the pricing and economics of Banking as a Service (BaaS – SaaS for banks) works.

The bank recognises that most activities outside direct servicing of the customer is commoditised. A commodity is worth nothing, and so all processing and technology is priced at near zero because they become freely available networked widgets.

Commodity processing being made freely available is a radical departure from bank histories which is why this will be a culture shock for many bankers ... and yet, the pricing and economics is relatively obvious.

Let's start with the cost of building BaaS.

The cost can be much you want it to be. In HSBC's case, the cost of building their global internet service is around $250 million ... but that's cheap enough considering that they were building a global bespoke service.

For HSBC that means they can launch a completely customised internet banking service in any country, by just ticking the boxes you want in that service and it's up and running. No additional development or cost.

But for most, it's not $250 million developments, it's a few thousand dollars to deploy a piece of functionality.

Y'see, the key point is that, whatever the cost is, once it's built, it's built. That's it. You have sunk the cost and built the widget.

Now, the critical point is not to protect the widget but to get everyone to use it. What's the point of investing in a development today if you can't get volume? And that's the point of BaaS: once you've built your widget, crank up the volume and volume increases fast these days.

That's how Chi-X, the pan-European equities trading facility, could take more than 10% of many traditional European exchanges equities trading ... within a year. And, having built the system, it is why Chi-x, Turquoise and NASDAQ OMX and co are after volume. It is why Zopa, SmartyPig and PayPal are leveraging volume.

And that's what any bank building components of applications should be thinking about today. Volume. Because additional volume adds zero cost and purely feeds return on investment.

Think of it like making movies. Once the movie is made, you've spent all the budget. Now, the point is to get bums on seats and market the hell out of it.

And that's how banking widgets in BaaS should be considered.

Market the hell out of your widget, crank up the volume and focus upon the service delivery – the human interfaces – as your critical value-add differentiation. Your value-add is how you package the widgets and present them, not the widgets themselves.

That's why Citigroup have been marketing the hell out of their FX and other services for the last two years. They want volume on their widget, and Citi are one of the few banks which have been white-labelling their systems to other banks. They get some of the BaaS components.

Which brings us back to the economics of banking in the future, under the BaaS model and the culture shock this creates.

I was recently with a head of payments at one bank for example, who said: "Our technology guys asked me the other day why we charge more for a $50 million payment than we do for a $5 payment, when the infrastructure costs to process are the same? Are they mad?"

No, sir. They are asking an obvious question at the heart of the change that needs to be made to banking cultures as they realise the change that technology now delivers.

This payments guy was from that old school of banking that are the ones now waking up to the new world realities.

Thirty years ago, when many senior bankers were starting out in their banks, they were told that technology was expensive, inflexible and must be used forever, or at least until the systems peg it anyway. That's why every project was massive, time-consuming and demanded huge cost.

When SWIFT, MasterCard, Visa and the key networks for transaction processing were built, for example, they had to be built by an industry consortium. No individual bank could afford such a huge project or cost. That is why these were cooperative groups back in the 1970s across all banks, even though MasterCard and Visa are now proprietary firms. Nevertheless, the MasterCard and Visa IPOs are only recent and recognise the economics of BaaS.

For example, back in 1975, the bank technology economic model was based on massive cost that slowly over time could be recouped through usage. Cost was depreciated slowly, and could only be covered by high prices and margins. Hence, banks, SWIFT and the card companies all worked hard to create the infrastructure, and cover the costs of that infrastructure through high transaction processing and interchange fees.

That was back then. This model had changed a little by 2000. What was happening in 2000, was that the post-Year 2000 hullaballoo was over. Many systems had been renovated and ration-

It's Banking Jim, But Not As We Know It

alised. And the costs of building new systems had reduced somewhat thanks to HTML (an internet language) and component/object-based modelling.

Therefore, banks found the time and cost of building new systems had been fundamentally reduced ... but the costs for usage and pricing did not come down as fast.

After all, if you've got a good thing, hold on to it! So the pricing and fee rates did not change dramatically, although we did see SWIFT's model changing.

For example, the then CEO of SWIFT, Leonard Schrank, was interviewed in 2003, and made a few statements about SWIFTNet was well underway using IP-based messaging, costs for a typical SWIFT message had come down 70% in the last decade, whilst volume had increased four-fold to 8 million messages per day.

What we were seeing a decade ago was that the cost to build was coming down, and volume was rising faster than before, thanks to ease of communication and connection.

SWIFT gave those savings back to their banking members, because they are bank-owned. However, banks have not yet passed all these cost reductions on to their clients but, thanks to today's competitive forces, they will.

Today, competitive forces recognise how the network has changed these pricing models even further.

Today, the cost to build should become virtually irrelevant if you are using the right tools but, once built, the volume can be cranked up really fast, thanks to openness, standards, ease of networking and communicating.

You see, the bottom line is that the economics of banking has fundamentally changed. This is because banking is based upon technology, and the economics of technology has fundamentally changed.

The new economics of banking: technology and systems, processing and functionality are virtually free; anything that is commodity activity should be brought in as a service and all pricing is for value-add, not commodities.

Today, it is a no-brainer to build new functionality, or even micro-functionality, and then deploy it openly, transparently and easily across the network.

That's why banking will be near-free.

It will be free because banks can build micro-functionality, widgets, and then make money out of volume. If I can get a thousand banks to serve a million companies processing a billion transactions through my banking widget of commoditised functionality, then I make money. And that process is far better than one bank working with a hundred firms to transact a thousand times through my very expensive and out-of-date legacy infrastructure.

The latter is the old way. Banking on the network is the new and better way.

And how do banks make money in this new world? By being the lowest cost integrator and offerer of the best white labelled banking widgets, and then charging me for advice and superior services to those commodity services offered by others.

This final part if where the culture shock will really hit.

In a world where every bank is offering transactions and processing for nothing, how can you make me feel you're so worthy as to be worth a fee?

The answer to that one is to focus upon the customer experience. The customer experience, service, dialogue and advice will become the critical differentiation and profit point.

Whoa ... now that's going to be tough isn't it?

Yep.

Collaborative competition (2009)

Let's look at collaborative technologies and, more specifically, collaborative competition.

It seems like an oxymoron to talk about collaborative competition and yet for years we talked about co-opetition, which is almost the same thing.

Cooperate or collaborate to compete implies both cartels and price fixing but, in today's reality, has nothing to do with this, or should not. Rather it's the idea of collaborating to improve business models through robust and reliable open source architectures, whilst identifying the components internally that differentiate within these collaborative models for competitive purposes.

Let's illustrate with an example that's top of the list today: risk.

When Lehmans collapsed last September, it happened to be the same day that the SIBOS conference started in Vienna. SIBOS had various themes and finished on the Thursday with a great presentation by Don Tapscott, the author of the book 'Wikinomics.'

Don talked about his whole approach to the social network stuff and the new age of the internet youth of digital natives, and illustrated the power of such thinking with a great story about writing his latest book.

Apparently he finished the book at Christmas time and asked his son what he thought of it. His son said that it didn't matter what he thought about it but what the collective view was, and offered to create a Facebook group to critique the book.

"Sure", says Dad and son dutifully created the group at lunchtime on Christmas Eve.

By the end of day, 300 teenagers amongst his son's peer group were actively reading, digesting, dissecting and critiquing the book such that, by Christmas Day, it had pretty much been re-written and was far better for it.

That's the power of the collective, the collaborative cohesion of the whole rather than the fragmented view of the one.

Now I know I'm starting to sound like someone writing about the Borg in Star Trek, and maybe I am, but I took on board Don's words, particularly his appeal at the end of his presentation.

Here's what he said:

"The risks in the financial system must be better managed in the future so why don't we create an open source group for risk managers? A Facebook for Risk Professionals, if you like. This group could then share and discuss risks in the financial systems and have contributions from all. Effectively, risk management becomes an open source arena so that everyone can build a more robust, reliable and resilient future."

Since he proposed such a system, what's happened?

Duh ... not much. Or not much in the risk management space that I can identify anyway. It seems we're all waiting for the governors to come up with their plans before implementing ours, but isn't that wrong?

Which brings it back to the theme of collaborative competition, which is another dimension of the new economics of banking.

Collaborative competition says that for things that are commodity or things that are industry wide issues and structures we should just widgetise and gadgetise, and make them plug and play processing capability and knowledge that is available to all.

These pieces add little value, are commoditised, should be free or near free, and paid for by ... advertising, or not at all.

That's the nature of collaboration. For example, through Google ads we can give away lots of knowledge and processing power, so why not have Google ads pay for banks' commodity processes and transactions.

Then, as a bank, you focus upon the bits where you differentiate. These are all the customer-centric parts of engagement, acquisition, delivery and fulfilment.

The result is that we could outsource compliance and plug AML/KYC into our client account opening processes by dropping in a cheap widget of functionality from a third party.

We could drop a gadget into our system for payments processing too – just use a white-labelled processor – and even find a wiki for a bit of credit risk management based upon an open source structure.

Then we provide a little bit of service improvement by offering SmartyPig as our savings vehicle for kids, for example, whilst focusing upon our own deployment of service around high-end wealth management for the kids' mums and dads.

The only bit of our banking operation we've developed and deployed in this model is wealth management servicing.

The rest – all the processing, compliance, risk and ancillary products – we've just dropped in as widgets of functionality into our banking structure. And those bits are all the bits of collaborative competition therefore.

We may compete with the providers of our widgets, but we also collaborate with them to use their processing where it makes sense or where it makes our own infrastructures more robust and reliable.

The result is that banking starts to look more and more like the car industry. A quarter of a century ago, car manufacturers prided themselves on having the best manufacturing. They produced all of the car's components and the manufacturer with the best components offered the most expensive cars. Today, nearly all cars are based upon standardised and commoditised manufacturing of the pieces. The manufacturer no longer manufactures, but just assembles the pieces into the whole and adds their own unique recipe of chassis and engine to differentiate.

BMW in 1980 manufactured thousands of unique components for their cars; today they just assemble them. But it's still BMW and the final product is still an aspirational brand that shows that they may use commodity components which VW, Ford and others use, but they assemble them into a brilliant car that swishes, swooshes and whizzes far more sleekly and smoothly than many others.

That's how banks will compete.

All the components they just get off the assembly line of banking functionality, but the banks that assemble them to address a specific target audience in the most appropriate way will win that audiences business.

Simple.

Chapter 3 Banking technology

Introduction

If you've been around banking for long, you will find there are a never-ending stream of technology firms offering software, hardware, networking and consulting services to get banks to adopt new capabilities. This is because banks are based around technology these days. Think about your bank: how much of the bank's relationship with you is reliant upon technology? For some, it is their complete relationship as they never visit a branch. This is true not just in retail banking, but also in investment banking where high frequency trading is in vogue. The bottom line is that banking is all about bits and bytes, so here's a few bits and bytes of banking technology developments to consider for the future.

What's in store for the technology of banking? (2010)

There are lots of questions about technology, such as:
- Will Google make us stupid?
- Will we live in the cloud or the desktop?
- Will social relations get better?
- Will the state of reading and writing be improved?
- Will online anonymity continue?
- Will the semantic web have an impact?

Lots of things we could talk about, but here are five key things that will happen in 2010 with banking technology:
- Banks will start using cloud computing services across the board;
- Real time becomes normal;
- Real time disrupts the status quo;
- Mobile services will continue to rip through banking and payments innovations;
- Contactless payments will finally start to make some inroads.

Banks will start using cloud computing services across the board

The use of cloud was a big discussion point through 2009, and I argued that many bank infrastructures could move to cloud-style services if they wanted to. But then some say cloud is just old-style mainframe computing, except that it has moved from the host controlled environment being private in-house to being public and open. Whatever.

The fact is that today's investment markets, due to latency requirements, are moving towards cloud for trade execution regardless. Proximity hosted, co-located servers will sit in massive server farms in Chicago, New York, London, Frankfurt, Mumbai, Shanghai, Hong Kong, Tokyo, Sao Paolo and other major trading cities, all connected by lightspeed communications, enabling global trading to take place faster than the blink of an eye. These comms lines already allow a global packet of trade data to move 32,000 kilometres around the world in less than 400 milliseconds (that's two really fast blinks of your eye) and networking firms tell me they will get these speeds down to under a millisecond by the end of this year/early next.

Therefore, the idea of having everything available through the Web on a secure plug and play connections anywhere, anytime (including on your mobile) will be the way to architect throughout 2010.

Real time becomes normal

With such lightning speeds, the idea of connecting and then having to wait three days or more for something to happen will become so last century. Banks that sit on funds for days will become targeted by consumers as weak banks. I mean, when you use a mobile phone to make a call, is it acceptable for the call to be answered in D+3? Send a tweet and get it 24 hours later? No

It's Banking Jim, But Not As We Know It

way. How long do you take to answer an email or get annoyed that someone hasn't responded to one (oh yes, and email is also way out of date – use Facebook and Twitter instead)?

So the idea of D+ or T+ is going to die a death in the 2010s, starting right now. Payments, transactions, cross-border money movements, fraud checks ... everything in banking will move to real time.

The real-time infrastructures will change the nature of banking and are of concern to some – "If we saw Lehmans collapse over weeks, what would happen if they could collapse in real-time" – but the movement to real time is inevitable and unstoppable.

However, the thing that goes with real-time money is real-time risk and real-time risk management. This is why real-time analytics and real-time reporting will become key. For example, the UK's FSA has already required trading firms in London to move towards real-time trade reporting, a move that will supposedly cost upwards of £2 billion to implement.

Real time disrupts the status quo

Now, real time doesn't necessarily mean that you give the customer real time. You might charge for real time or near real time, and that's where it gets interesting. After all, if you can process a payment of £100 million for the same price and in the same speed as a £1 payment, then where is the bank adding value?

Equally, infrastructures that inhibit real time – such as the complexity of SWIFT messaging around transactions – may start to call into question the raison d'être of those infrastructures. SWIFT has been challenged many times over its raison d'être – Heidi Miller asked in 2004: "If the internet is ubiquitous and free, why should we pay SWIFT for messaging?" – and they've continued to innovate and push for change through SWIFTNet and XML messaging.

Now, however, the community-based infrastructures of the past – created due to the cost barriers of implementing technology in the 1970s on a global scale – are no longer necessary. This is why Visa and MasterCard IPO'd, and why community infrastructures will give way to open infrastructures with secure networking layers.

This last point will be a critical challenge to SWIFT and others – the London Stock Exchange, for example – in 2010, and will see further upset of the status quo.

Mobile services will continue to rip through banking and payments innovations

One of my favourite subjects of 2009 was the mobile telephone as an interface to the bank. This was particularly down to the fact that 2009 was the year that mobile internet became easy thanks to the iPhone.

The iPhone will transform banking generally, and is already proving to be a killer app for finance thanks to iPhone apps. iPhone apps abound for finances. Banks have started rushing out iPhone apps too, with NatWest being one of the first UK banks to major on this, although BBVA, Bank of America and others have been on the case for a while now.

But the transformation starts to happen when you see innovators like Twitter co-founder Jack Dorsey starting to think about using the iPhone as a payments system.

This is his new venture Square, a simple clip-on to the iPhone headset jack that turns the phone into a payments processing machine. Jack's is a heavy US-centric view of the payments world and what he doesn't know is that the mag stripe and signature is also so last century.

It's Banking Jim, But Not As We Know It

Contactless payments will finally start to make some inroads.

We're now into contactless cards and Chip & PIN. For a while, contactless has been discussed and hasn't really taken off. This is no reflection on the banks, as several have tried to rollout major programmes such as the Chase Blink Card and Barclaycard OnePulse. Barclaycard recently reached 5 million cards issued, for example, but that still doesn't make this a major success ... yet.

The reason is not enough places to use a contactless card. But that's changing.. Suddenly, bringing together the mobile phone with apps that turn it into a point-of-sale doesn't seem stupid or strange ... it just makes sense. Like Jack Dorsey's Square, turning the mobile into a payments system for both transmitting and receiving money is not the future ... it is here and now.

And that's what we will see more of in 2010. More innovations on the mobile internet to make money on a mobile as easy as cash in your pocket.

Now that makes 2010 a very exciting year, doesn't it?

Let the iWars begin ... (2010)

(...)

Here's a vision of the future based upon the logic is that banks are being componentised. As banks componentise their services into little pieces of functionality, my original proposal is that they would then offer these as widgets to customers who could build them back into any form of integrated service they wanted.

Now, my view has gone a step further with the belief that the banks will actually wrap them into apps. I should say that my use of the word app here, is in terms of the ease-of-use of Apple apps but it does not mean that has to be Apple-based.

Just so you know I'm not an Apple fanatic, just someone who can see the ease-of-use of apps is a revolution. So where I talk about apps, think about Google's Android phone or any other phone that makes mobile internet access easy, as these are the new generations of phone that are revolutionary.

Y'see first there were SMS and WAP-based phones; then there were mobile internet access smartphones; and now there are intelligent mobile internet phones with apps.

That's the revolution.

The first phones were mainly for just that – telephone calls. The second wave allowed us to pull information to the phone, but push internet services were more difficult. Push began with the Blackberry, but that was just for push email. The iPhone revolution of apps gives us location-based push services that users download to gain such usability.

That's the revolution.

It gives us the ability to create location-based components of functionality that are relevant at the point of action. It gives users the immediate access to pieces of functionality on demand. It makes using the internet on the mobile as simple as touching a screen.

That's the revolution.

Now, back to banking and treasury services.

If banks are component-based, and each bank offers different treasury apps and usability, you will soon end up with a million banking apps. There will be a liquidity risk app, an e-invoicing app, a supply chain app, a cash management app, an accounts payable app, a foreign exchange app ... and so on and so forth.

Corporates will then take these apps and select those that work best for their businesses. They will download the apps to their corporate treasury iPads, iPhones and Androids (Google), and roll these out to their employees who need to look at days sales outstanding, inventory, supplies and logistics, etc. These employees will be used to the interface and service – a bit like

It's Banking Jim, But Not As We Know It

folks got used to using PCs and keyboards to access the internet in the old days – and will take to this easily.

Similarly, the users, the corporates and the banks will be in continual 'synch' because, just as my iPhone automatically synched with my iTunes and Outlook, it will automatically synch with my corporate treasury processes, data and content.

In other words, you end up with treasury being redefined as we move to banking-on-demand 24-7 through treasury-in-the-pocket.

The critical point in this logic is that, by making treasury app-based, corporates will be much more efficient:

- They will be able to mix and match the apps and the app providers – banks – to best fit their business model;
- They will be able to ensure that even the most unskilled member of staff, associate, player, employee or whatever can use them;
- They can be easily adjusted to suit business changes over time through centralised control;
- They can be a mix of in-house created or bank provided and operated or collegiate, open source apps; and
- They will always be secure, up-to-date, controlled and managed in real time 24-7.

All of the above will give the treasury ops incredible flexibility, agility and speed to adapt to changing circumstances.

So here's the proposed treasury operations future. The corporate treasury runs on SAP today, and will in the future probably. However, the CFO will have consolidated all treasury ops onto SAP as a single platform and determined that a small number of bank partners will be selected to integrate with it.

Those bank partners will be selected on the basis of the beauty, ease, adaptability and refreshment of their component-based bank app functionality, and its fit with the business needs of the corporation.

To me, this is a simplified future as we have turned a tipping point from proprietary bank lock in and lack of standards in the past, to very easy and flexible developments that are open sourced and simple in the future.

And here's where I got shot down at the conference in Asia I was attending.

"Oh, but treasury is far more complex than your simple consumer view of the future."

"Oh, but this won't work because our processes and infrastructures are too difficult to change to this vision."

"Oh, but technology is expensive."

"Oh, but oh but, oh but, yea but no but yea but no ..."

I was really disappointed with this reaction; I expected more buy-in for such a vision in visionary Asia.

Then I got it. None of these guys in developing Asian markets use iPhones.

The thing that really sticks in the throat is that by omitting to view these developments, corporates and banks will miss the whole trend towards business simplification that such tools allow.

Luckily some banks are not so short-sighted in Asia, as the announcement of the iPad coming up for sale from July in Singapore was underscored with the news that OCBC and DBS have both developed specific apps for this service, amongst the first.

Meanwhile, and to put the record straight, HSBC and First Direct are on the case with these technologies as they are sponsors of this conference and have told me some of their plans.

Finally, and the real underline of this blog entry, is that it now explains why, when the Chair of the panel I was on asked: "Chris, what are the new things you see happening? Do you think, for

It's Banking Jim, But Not As We Know It

example, that we could use the iPhone for Treasury one day?", he got a big laugh with that opening question.

These guys think the iPhone is just a toy. It's not. The iPhone, Android and, more importantly, the app is for business use as much as it is for consumers.

Get real.

Postnote: it's a shame but I suspected this at the time. Apparently many folks in the audience thought that I was some Appleite with iPhomania because I kept referring to 'apps'. To be honest, I meant apps as an interchangeable idea with widgets and gadgets to refer to the componentised bank functions.

It actually doesn't matter that much if folks did interpret this as being Apple-based, however, as the PC age was Microsoft-based, the internet-age is Google/Firefox/Explorer-based and the mobile internet is now Apple-based.

With 100 million units shipped in just three years, a further 58 million this year, the iPhone is becoming the de facto standard for the mobile internet.

Ah, but wait, what's this?

> "Android tops iPhone: Google's Android operating system edged out Apple's iPhone operating system for the No. 2 spot in the US consumer smartphone market in the first quarter, according to research firm NPD Group."

Whatever.

Why would a bank change its core system? (2010)

There are lots of reasons why a bank would change its core system. Here's my top five.

Legacy constraints

This is the most obvious one, but it does not create a reason for changing a core system in or of itself. After all, I know of plenty of banks that continue to operate processors and applications developed in the 1960s and 1970s because the view is: 'if it ain't broke, leave it'. That's why many City institutions still have a need for FORTRAN and ASSEMBLER programmers, and why some banks process transactions converted to pounds, shillings and pence (pre-decimal systems should have been dropped in 1971!). It is because these systems worked and were too expensive to change back in the 1970s and 1980s. Now, 50 years later, they have the problem that they are too incomprehensible to change. After all, many of the folks who developed these systems didn't document them and the developers are now retired, suffering from dementia or dead. So the bank keeps them running as they can't dump them. However, if the legacy is causing them to be uncompetitive and to lose business, then that may finally prompt the change of core system that has been so strategically required for decades but ignored. This leads us to the next major reason for change: competitors.

Competition

A bank will often change systems if competitive pressures force it to. For example, no bank wanted to launch call centre or online banking services until someone launched it first and started taking accounts away from them. This is why banks are variously described as sheep or lemmings, because they all follow each other around and copy what each other is doing. The result is that if a new core system capability delivers significant competitive differentiation for a financial institution, then all the other institutions will either buy the same system, buy a similar one from the provider's competitors or will copy it.

It's Banking Jim, But Not As We Know It

Regulations

All of the regulations that have been introduced over the past few years such as MiFID, the PSD, Faster Payments, the Capital Requirements Directive, RegNMS, MT202 Cover Payments and more, have required significant change to systems, structure and processes for the banks and operators in those market sectors impacted. Therefore, every time there's a legislative change, it will more than likely prompt an assessment as to the fitness for purpose of the existing system to meet and comply with the new obligation and, if it doesn't comply or if it is too difficult to adapt, then the bank will change core system.

Merger and acquisition

Every time a bank merger occurs, there has to be a rationalisation of systems as that is a core rationale for justification of a merger. In other words, cost savings... there is absolutely no rhyme or reason as to why a bank would run two parallel core systems as that would mean twice the cost. Therefore, one of the core systems will change. Unfortunately, it usually means that the core system changes by throwing out the system of the acquired bank and converting it across to the acquirer's platforms. This has little to do with effectiveness or efficiency and is more to do with ego and power. For example, NatWest's systems were forced onto Royal Bank of Scotland's when RBS took over NatWest a decade ago and, more recently, Abbey's were dumped and converted to Santander's. In retrospect, it would make more sense for a fuller review to take place before such decisions are made to ask: (a) which is the best system, and (b) is there a better one outside the bank overall? Having said that, I cannot imagine any bank converting both their own and their acquired bank's systems across to a new platform at the same time but, when acquiring a bank, it would be a good time to consider converting the acquired bank's core system to the best in the market and, if that means buying externally, then convert your own core systems across to the same platform thereafter.

New management

Again, it is often just a case of ego and power, but when new management takes over a bank, the first thing they want to do is to stamp their authority on it. This can be done in two ways: first, sack all of the sycophants who worked for the previous management team; second, replace all of their decisions with new ones that show how ineffective their decisions were. The latter means finding things they did or did not do, and then showing how stupid they were. For example, not replacing an old legacy system may be a good way to highlight this; or the fact that they replaced core systems but didn't choose a good one is another. Either way, a new management team, given the right prodding, could easily be convinced to change core systems if they thought the previous management had been shirking their responsibilities by not changing it or changing it for a poorer one.

So there you have five good reasons to change core systems: legacy constraints, competitive forces, regulatory mandate, merger and acquisition and new management requirements.

Thinking about these things, the post-crisis fallout means that all of the above are rife. Many banks have new management teams, are going through a tumultuous acquisition, have been forced to change due to regulation, and have new competitors and new customer needs that put a strain on their legacy operations. This means that 2010 onwards is a great time to see core systems change in many European and American banks.

However, there's one point that is not made above that is just as critical. No bank will change a core system because of new technology.

New technologies are great. They may be sexy, interesting, create differential and be very compelling, but new technologies in and of themselves will never justify a core systems change.

It is only when the new technology can demonstrate that it will support the needs to be compliant with new legislation; or to eradicate legacy overhead for operational efficiency; or to improve management and business processes that the bank can maintain competitive parity now and into the future; that the systems are purchased.

In other words, the debate about core systems has nothing to do with the features and functionality of the technology itself, but is triggered by a burning platform that means that if the bank does not change the core system they will flounder.

That is the key to why banks change core systems and the sooner providers get off the feature, functionality and technology platform and get on to the business need, management drivers and strategic platforms, the better.

Technology is key for banking (2009)

I found a whole range of technology predictions for 2009. One of the best general forecasts comes from Gartner, which says that the top 10 technology areas to focus upon during an economic crisis are:

1. Reduce headcount or freeze hiring;
2. Renegotiate with technology and service providers;
3. Curtail data centre expansion, virtualise assets and lease them back;
4. Consolidate systems;
5. Outsource commodity;
6. Offshore outsource;
7. Investment shutdown;

8. Prioritise projects;
9. Mothball businesses and projects;
10. Change leadership and restructure IT teams.

I agree with this list.

In banking, it goes further. In banking, technology is a critical part of the solution for the crisis, and technology also provides a way to avoid the crisis occurring again. That is why I titled this as technology providing 'a key for banking in 2009'.

Technology is the key. It is a method of solving the market issues long-term – if deployed correctly – and banks, governments and corporations will realise this in 2009.

Five banking technology forecasts for 2009

2009 will be a year for introspection and circumspection rather than innovation and action. This means that the majority of banks will focus upon highly conservative cost saving projects with short-term returns on investment. The long-term and strategic will be dropped by many, as will the regulatory. That's why some key milestones will be missed, particularly for the Payments Services Directive in Europe. After all, what is the point of implementing regulatory change in a year when all regulations are likely to change?

Banks will avoid anything discretionary, anything uncertain, anything unnecessary and anything intangible, so here are the top five things that all banks will focus upon as a result:

1) Systems rationalisation

Server consolidation, virtualisation and grid technologies will also be a critical aspect of improving services and streamlining costs. Banks will see the reduction of distributed servers and data centres, to consolidation into a few centres as being a key focal point. This is demonstrated best by HSBC.

It's Banking Jim, But Not As We Know It

In 2003, the bank had 130 data centres in over 80 countries. By 2008, they had rationalised these centres down to just 20, and aim to reduce this to six by 2010. Why? Because the bank is run on the network and large data centres provide global platforms for reducing costs, focusing skills in a few centres of excellence, improving resilience and capabilities through economies of scale, and allowing any new regional or local business to be established rapidly and easily by just layering them upon the network.

These are critical aspects for all banks to focus upon in 2009.

2) Outsourcing

We have seen a move to offshoring and outsourcing for many banks over the past few years, but 2009 will see a major increase in the focus of moving non-strategic services out of the organisation in an effort to reduce costs. The typical areas will include core applications maintenance, ATM network management, server management, co-location and proximity services. Equally, as more mergers and acquisitions occur, expect to see the acquired operations being moved out of the bank to outsourcing partners.

3) Networking

As HSBC's Ken Harvey stated, the "network is the bank". Banks that are not running on hi-speed bandwidth will be challenged as speed is a critical differentiator. Low latency in the investment markets for speed of trade execution through to leveraging web technologies for better customer service in the retail markets will be seen as a critical and core competence. Therefore, all banks will see this as priority.

4) Interoperability and standards

But it's more than speed, it's connectivity. Connectivity between banks, between banks and corporations, between banks and consumers and, most importantly, between banks and regulators will mean that interoperability and standards will come to the fore. Although interoperability has been discussed for years, the

64

fact that it is still non-existent in many areas of the markets is now a known weakness.

Therefore, regulatory authorities will rapidly move towards a fully connected marketplace globally where all monetary movements and financial instruments are connected and visible, rather than opaque or transparent. This will be seen as a critical G20 change programme, and will rise to top the agenda by end of year. Banks that are not on global standards and networks will be seen as non-compliant.

5) Risk management

The last two points build to the final point: the connectivity of bank systems through real-time networks will be seen as a key driver and motivator in order to provide effective industry risk management.

I actually wrote about this back in September 2007, where I discussed the issues Lloyd's of London faced when ineffective risk management hit the market. The issue then was that risk was leaving Lloyd's through reinsurers who then reinsured back into Lloyd's. Result: the majority of risk lay with a few key players in the market who collapsed when catastrophic risks occurred.

In banking, this is exactly what has happened in the 2000s, even though it is lending rather than risk. The issue is that leveraged lending allowed banks to create liquidity that did not exist. Result: the majority of leverage lay with a few key players in the market who collapsed when liquidity disappeared.

What did Lloyd's do?

They created a run-off company, Equitas, that took all the toxic risk from the market and managed it in a long-tail trade-off firm, whilst creating a centralised risk system where all firms logged their underwriting. The latter allowed the supervisory administration of Lloyd's to see the total risk portfolio across the market and the exposures of each firm. Any firm that over-leveraged their

It's Banking Jim, But Not As We Know It

risks were curtailed, such that the catastrophic risk exposures that hit the market in the 1980s would never happen again.

What will the banking system do? Give the governments all their toxic financial instruments whilst creating a centralised real-time risk system to ensure this never happens again. The real-time exchange will log financial instruments being traded by whom with whom. The real-time system will also log the total capital of the institutions involved against their portfolio of risk, borrowing and trading, to see their total leverage position. Firms will be provided with leverage and capital limits as an enhancement to Basel, which will be managed in real time.

Effectively, governments, banks and corporations will all be connected to a massive data warehouse which runs a global real-time risk exchange. And I would propose that the DTCC, now that they have LCH.Clearnet and EuroCPP in their camp, are well positioned to provide this.

Either way, the capability to focus upon networks, interoperability and standards in 2009, combined with regulatory changes that enforce the centralisation of risk management in a real-time system, will provide one cornerstone towards the long-term solution for this crisis.

Meantime, these five areas of technology operations will be the focal points for all banks in 2009.

(...)

IT architectures: why technologists have lost the plot (2008)

It's really tough dealing with technologists. It is like the old discussion of the businessman in the hot-air balloon who is lost. He spies a chap on the ground and asks if he knows where he is. The guy looks up and says, "You are about 35 feet in the air, supported by a vehicle comprising cloth and ropes, and filled with helium." The business man looks puzzled and says, "You must be a technologist." "Wow", the guy says. "I am. How did you know?" "Because what you have told me is technically accurate, but of absolutely no use to anyone." "Ah", says the guy. "You must be a businessman." "I am", says the businessman, "but how did you know?" "Because I was minding my own business and you asked me to help you out, so I gave you assistance in the best way I could, and now you blame me for the mess you're in."

Ouch. Business and technology folks really don't get on well.

The reason I raise this today is because I spent yesterday with a bunch of technologists. The focus of the discussion was SOA – Service Oriented Architecture.

Is that Customer Service Oriented Architecture, I hear you ask? No, it's Web Service Oriented Reusable Objects for Interoperability Architectures.

Oh dear. At this point, most business people have left the room.

Now, I think I know what they were trying to say, as I used to be a programmer, but if I were a business person then I'd probably have no idea what they were talking about because you end up using a bunch of acronyms and words from foreign lands, such as SOA, SOAP, J2EE, BPEL, XML, CDL, MDDL, FpML ... you name it.

No wonder business folks would rather smell a monkey's armpit than talk to a technologist.

The real point is that through SOA, firms claim you have re-usability of code to be more agile through being able to plug and play and evolve into highly flexible systems.

Apparently, according to the technologists, no business person wants to hear the plea for investment in this stuff, however. Investing in building future, flexible architectures for their technology operations just falls on deaf ears. As a result, they tell me

It's Banking Jim, But Not As We Know It

that SOA is an IT investment, not a business investment. Business people don't want to hear about it, and so it's snuck in under the regulatory change, compliance and discretionary investment budgets. There is no budget for 're-architecting' the bank.

I do not like that view, as I think SOA should be a business dialogue and investment, not something hidden under the radar.

What the business people need are business conversations.

First, a business discussion around why SOA is felt to be important.

Second, a business discussion about why SOA will deliver business benefits.

Neither of these discussions normally comes up with a technology group because we talk about objects, modules, standards and technologies. However, there is a business dialogue that could be proposed, and it would go something like this.

First, how to position SOA for the business crowd.

Well, imagine you are building a house. Most house builders employ architects to ensure the foundations and structures are right. Most house builders also employ one architect, not many. So you first of all need an enterprise architect to create the overall architecture for the bank's systems.

Relating this to house building, you cannot have multiple architects as then the doors and windows, joists and beams might all be different. Sure, if you want a quirky house then that is fine but, if you want a great house, you give the job to a single expert architect.

So that's what we need in a systems context.

We've built many systems over the past 50 years without an architect involved. Designers and developers for sure, but house designers and developers create buildings that are inappropriate for secure long-term structures.

This is the point of SOA. It allows us to create a technology house built as a long-term secure structure for the bank, rather than some higgledy-piggledy labyrinth.

The reason why this is important today is that we now have technologies that conform to international standards. In other words, if our systems were built like a house today, we would be using global standards for cement, bricks and glass, whereas much of what we had before was built using local materials that were good, but not for global structures.

We have global structures and this means we can rationalise into a global architecture using standardised materials. That's why we need an enterprise architecture, an enterprise architect, and a clear long-term secure technology infrastructure to evolve the bank into the future with agility, flexibility and simplicity.

The second piece of the dialogue is that, if we did this, what's the benefit to the bank?

This should again be clear, and it's not woolly benefits about re-usability and agility. Nope, it's about reduced cost and increased revenues. Using standard materials means that if you've created a program for a card payment once, for example, you can use that program again and again and again. A little like if you manufacture a 6x4 glass window frame once, you can manufacture that frame 1,000 times for zero cost overhead. That's what we can do today with systems.

And that's the real point. Scale efficiency, standardised materials, re-usability and repeatability. This way you minimise costs and maximise returns. Before, many banks had systems that hinder efficiency because they used non-standard materials and cannot be re-used, replaced or redesigned easily. So what we had before maximised costs and minimised returns. That's why we need to re-architect.

It's Banking Jim, But Not As We Know It

In this context, an illustration of approach with results always helps, so I'll pick on HSBC's CIO, Ken Harvey, who was interviewed by *Financial Services Technology* magazine in May 2008.

In the article, it states that he was "tasked by the Board with the goal of cutting HSBC's unit processing costs by 10 per cent each year, and managing an annual IT budget of around £2.5 billion." This led to a complete redesign and rationalisation of HSBC's global systems infrastructures and applications, with results that leverage global scale. Mr. Harvey states that the "benefit has been 85 per cent on the revenue generation side, with only 15 per cent on the cost reduction side."

The whole point is that, by rationalising systems and making them reusable, you can scale the efficiencies and leverage the capabilities of a single design, many times.

I'm not saying that this discussion resolves the fact that technologists and business folks don't get on well, nor that SOA is the right and only way forward, but technology folks should realise that by sneaking IT rationalisation into the IT budget, they are missing a trick.

The trick they are missing is that they are behaving as a silo function without getting business buy-in. Without business commitment, IT investments such as SOA, will just be some half-cut, half-hearted effort, rather than realising the results that could have been unleashed if this was delivered by the enterprise, for the enterprise.

What is 'world-class technology'? (2008)

(...)

World-class technology has five key attributes, and possibly more, but these are the five we came up with in a recent discussion

First, the investment should enhance the business. It should deliver benefits that are measurable and improve cost-income ratio in some form.

Second, the technology should deliver an enhanced experience for the user, and especially for the customer if the technology is customer visible.

Customers want to see the bank as being different, and technology can create differentiated propositions. As most customers connect with the bank most of the time through technology, this is especially true today. So the investment should have a visible impact on the customer. We also noted that 'customer' included both internal and external users, not just the final customer.

Third, that experience and change must be consistent. The technology must not disrupt other channels, unless it replaces them of course, but should be consistently adding value to the bank and the bank's client relationship. Anything that would create a noticeable chasm between current state and future state is not world class.

Fourth, it should be future-proofed. Whatever technology a bank buys these days, should have the ability to incorporate any changes to business, products, services, technologies, infrastructure, operations ... you name it. That's a tough call and Service Oriented Architecture (SOA) tries to answer it, although no-one was convinced that SOA was the answer.

Lastly, it should be delivering the future. This was pointing at technology trends coming downstream, such as the Semantic Web, and saying that the technology procured today should already be incorporating key features of these developments to be world class.

You may think this is the same as the last point, but the difference is that the last point is protecting the investment whereas being future-ready is saying that the investment includes some

It's Banking Jim, But Not As We Know It

of the required future capabilities anticipated, rather being about protecting the investment. It's a nuance I know, but we felt it was an important one.

I'm sure there's more in this, so feel free to add your own views, but if you used these five criteria:

- ◆ Does this technology deliver a clear and measurable business benefit?
- ◆ Will it enhance the user's experience?
- ◆ Is this something that is consistent with our current state and, if not, what are the implications?
- ◆ Is the technology future-proofed? and
- ◆ Does this technology help us to deliver the future?,

then it's not a bad acid test when making IT investments. Not exhaustive, but a good start.

Chapter 4 **The great channel debate**

Introduction

Until recently, banking was 100% focused upon branch distribution. This was down to the fact that no-one thought people would deal with banks without branches. The first bank to break this mould was First Direct. Then we found internet banking evolved things further, with Bank of America supporting over 25 million customers via such services and, more recently, banks such as Jibun Bank in Japan have emerged that are just mobile-only based banks. The debate this creates is two-fold: first, are branches still needed, and second, can banks really succeed at being multi-channel or are banks only successful as mono-channel? The latter question is really interesting for me, as I cannot name a bank that is superb across all channels. They tend to excel at one and are then mediocre to poor in the others. Nevertheless, excelling at all channels you deploy will be key to the future bank, and that's the debate that really needs to take place.

The branch-based banking model is dead (2009)

The traditional model of banking is dead: long live the new bank model. The dead model is the one where 80% of costs of retailing are in stores (branches).

Branch-based banking is dead. Branches are not dead ... just the concept of branch-based banking per se. You still need some branches for sales and relationships. But about a tenth of the number that most banks have today, as the majority are just administration or transaction outlets that can be automated.

The point is that 8 out of 10 branches were opened as administration centres to service the transaction needs of communities. Those needs are now being self-serviced, so what are those transaction centres there for?

In particular, as 95% of customer contact is now being delivered remotely through technology channels, including corporate customers, this should mean that at least 80% of the cost goes into the staffing, processes and technology used in those channels. In other words, 80% of the old bank operational costs for retailing were in branches. Today, it should be in technology channels.

But there's more to it than that. It's about relationship and connections.

People get technology today, not because it's gadgets but because it is connecting their lives to the lives of countless friends and strangers. This is why Facebook can go from nothing to a place with the population of the United States in under four years, and why Twitter can go from off-the-radar to on everyone's radar in just under a year. Last year, no-one mentioned Twitter. Today, it's an integral part of the show. But it's only integral because it helps people manage, share and organise their lives and loves.

And that's what banks have to do if they are to reconnect. They must connect people to their money and finances in a simple and easy way.

A little more explanation of the flow. To start with, today's kids see the computer and its operating system as a history lesson. They don't care how technology works, just as I don't care how electricity works. I just like what it can do, and that's how kids see technology.

They also see banks as a history lesson. Their grandparents went into branches, their parents used ATMs and they just think of money and banking as being like Mint, an internet service that organises their finances for them. What's a bank branch for, therefore?

Equally, everyone keeps referring to the Facebook and Twitter generation, or the twitfaced generation as some might call them. Who are the twitfaced generation? They're not the under 25s. They're not the under 35s. They are the over 35s. Most Facebook

It's Banking Jim, But Not As We Know It

and Twitter users are average age of 40. So when we talk about social networks, we are not talking about the next generation of customers. We are talking about the current generation.

If anything, the new generation of customers should be called 'the Mob', as they are all about being mobile connected youth.

So what we're really saying is that you need to completely rethink the bank around social technologies and rethink the branch network by closing most of it down and reinvesting that saving into social finance.

If you don't, you're dead. Give it less than a decade, and you're dead. I'm serious.

Mainstream media fought this battle ... and lost. That's why television and newspapers are shutting down by the bucket load as today's media is created by me on YouTube and Typepad.

So stop fighting the lost bank cause of the branch network.

Rethink it. Keep the branches you need for sales, and shut the rest down. Replace them with ATMs. Equally, start thinking about new ideas such as micro-transactions. A billion iPhone app downloads in nine months. Charge 50 cents a download and you've generated $500 million. That's the future. It's the grains of sand that will build the future.

And some banks get this stuff. eBank and Jibun Bank in Japan; Wells Fargo and Bank of America in the US; BBVA, Caja Navarro and a few others in Europe; but these are few and far between.

In summary, the bank of the future will connect with me intimately via my mobile lifestyle 24-7. They will not only be proactive, but predictive of my needs and will provide me with a connection not just to a payment or to my money, but to my financial lifestyle.

That's what MINT is doing today and BBVA has delivered too, but it requires bravery to go down this route.

Being brave by shutting down transaction centres, opening hi-tech 21st century sales centres and pushing the rest down a common technology platform that supports access via mobile, laptop, music player, television, car ... any internet-enabled device, basically.

And this changes your business model, as the old model would involve massive investment in the business case to launch new technology platforms.

Today, technology is free and disposable.

So get on with it. Retail bankers of the world, unite. Shut down the branches and bite the bullet. Stop fighting the old fight and start focusing on the future.

Otherwise you're just dead meat, and who are we all going to sell to then?

The mobile phone companies?

Branch-based banking is dead, Part Two (2009)

A few folks seem to disagree with my assertion that branch-based banking is dead, but they may have misinterpreted my assertion as being branches are dead. They're not. Branches are very much alive and kicking ... just not as transaction centres. Branches are sales centres. And it is for this reason that the current branch system is dead, long live the new branch system.

It's very much in keeping with the realignment of the other industries, for example, book, record and travel shops, where their customers too have gone online and become self-serving.

It's a lesson banks are learning. The lesson is that this is broken, just like the old record store and book shop distribution system is dead. The result is that most banks will eventually rationalise down to just one store for every 250,000 people – or one store for every large town, city and shopping mall – rather than the current structure where this is about one store for every 20,000 people.

It's Banking Jim, But Not As We Know It

So what do you do with 80% of stores that are no longer needed? The ones that are in suburbs and smaller main streets. You ditch them. You substitute them with satellite self-service hub stations where folks self-serve with ATMs and deposit machines.

These hubs don't disconnect the customer from the human face of the banks as, if you want to talk to a human, then there would be a remote advisor station in the ones that have larger footfall. A video terminal for access to advice.

And if you want to talk to a real human, you would be offered an appointment-making facility where someone could visit you either at home or work.

So that's the bank distribution of the future.

80% or more of existing branches close down and are replaced by machines. 20% are relocated into the best shop and work locations, and become cool mega branches for sales and advice, modelled around genius bars and yes, a place that encourages you to come in and relax over a cappuccino whilst talking about your money.

That still holds true.

Many banks are implementing the strategy above as we speak ... whilst some poor countries are left with an affliction called the old bank model ,with management too worried about operational expense to see the bigger picture.

The problem being that if they don't re-architect their branch network, then they will be walking the path of Woolworths (one of UK's largest and oldest retailers: born 1909, died 2009).

Note: This primarily focuses upon economies where the cost of physical distribution is high due to staff and building costs. It does not necessarily apply to countries where it is cheaper to run a branch operation than an IT operation.

Branches wanted – dead or alive? (2009)

There are wide differences of opinion between different banks of the role of a branch these days.

Is a branch a branch, a store, a transactional centre, a sales centre, a retail lobby, an automated machine or all of these things or none of them?

On the one hand, I see HSBC saying that branches are uneconomic; on the other hand, Santander has decided to rebrand all their UK branches and want more. Meanwhile, there are new banks opening branches, such as Tesco and Metro Bank, and old banks closing branches by the dozen.

Who is right and who is wrong? Are branches alive and kicking, dead and gone, or in terminal decline? Answer: depends where you sit.

A branch is useful for banks that see them as a key channel and as an asset for human interfacing. Many want branches around as a place to go to ensure the bank can be trusted and to talk to someone. The ability to transact and interact with a human.

But, yet again, you don't need branches for that either, do you? You can interact with humans on telephones, via keyboard and, soon, via remote video.

So what is the real point of a branch?

It's ... errrr ... it's to ... to errrr ... it's to sell, isn't it?

The future bank will have big sales centres replacing existing branches, and then lots of automated satellite stations for transaction services.

No. Rubbish. You can sell via the internet and telephone too. After all, if you needed branches then no-one would bank with call-centre only banks such as First Direct.

So, what is the real point of a branch?

It's Banking Jim, But Not As We Know It

It's a channel. And, if you are a bank that sees the human channel with physical connectivity as being important, as Santander obviously do, then you need branches.

If you are a bank that sees remote connectivity and services with limited human interaction in a physical space, as HSBC see the world, then you do not need branches ... just automated transaction centres.

And customers will self-select their preferred bank to service them based upon their view of the bank's competence at managing these channels and the channels they offer that suit the customer's lifestyle.

So, if I'm a customer who wants a bank with branches and humans, then I will choose between Santander and the few other banks on Main Street left to service me that way.

Meantime, if I'm a customer who never wants to see a branch again in their lifetime, then give me First Direct, Smile, PayPal, Zopa and SmartyPig any day.

This is the reason why Metro Bank and Tesco are getting into UK bank branches ... because they recognise that the incumbent players have no idea as to whether to be committed or de-committed to their branch strategies and operations.

And while the incumbents dither and prevaricate, they are just losing on both ends of the scale. Their customers are dissatisfied with their shoddy, under-invested branch operations, and their competitors are seeing huge opportunities to recreate the branch experience to gain traction with those customers who want a branch experience.

No wonder banking is such fun when the business models are being reconstructed in real time and the decision makers haven't noticed or reacted.

To dump or not to dump the branch (2007)

I never knew how much debate could be created by making the mere statement of placing IP-enabled networks at the core of the bank and re-engineering to exploit this as the basis of future banking. This is instead of placing branch networks at the core.

Some people believe this is purely academic as we have branches today and can't get rid of them, so the question is how to use the branches we have today.

My contention is different.

As I have stated many times before, branches are critical sales centres and, in the future, they will not be transaction centres. Historically, they have been transaction centres. This is what everyone is struggling with today: how to turn tellers into sellers and branches into sales operations.

Personally, I don't think you can turn tellers into sellers. It's a bit like turning credit risk officers into customer service reps ... it may work with a few, but most would rather be credit risk officers and tellers.

So you firstly need to rehire.

If you are going to do that, then you also need to ask in the transformation process, that if you are going to turn your old transactional branches into sales operations, do you need so many of them? If you get rid of the transaction focus and move it to machines on the high street or in a branch lobby, how many branches do you then need?

Equally, if you are moving branches away from transactions, which are now managed through remote telephone and internet connections and other self-service machines, all of which are IP-enabled systems including the branch ATMs, then how do you rethink the network?

It's Banking Jim, But Not As We Know It

Those who think branches are the start point will throw good money after bad. Those who think IP networks are the start point, and then build the end-points (which include branches) on top, will be much nearer the right strategy for the future.

I'm sure folks will carry on arguing this point – after all, I run workshops on this stuff and make a good living out of it (as do many others) – but I know for a fact that those who think IP networks are just layered on top of old infrastructures, networks, distribution strategies and organisations are wrong. Afer all, having been around re-engineering bank processes for over two decades, this is why we have ended up with silo structures, painful processes and inappropriate skills.

So, in summary, my point is that the strategy needs to start around an IP-enabled bank. If you were designing that bank, then here's the question I would ask around the branch focus:

♦ How many branches would you layer on top?
♦ How many of those would be self-service automated branches and how many would be sales centres?
♦ How many staff, and what sort of staff, would you hire for those sales centres?
♦ What would be the customer demographics for each sales centre, and how would those staff skills fit with those customers?
♦ What happens to the existing staff and who do you need to reskill or offer severance?
♦ What are the technological aspects of the IP-enabled branch in this context, and how much technology do you put into the branch?
♦ What is that technology doing and how does it profile against the staff skills and customer demographics?
♦ Is the technology future-proofed and how engaging is this going to be, versus putting that service into other channels such as online or through contact centres?

- How does the underpinning of the new IP-enabled branch fit with the IP-enabled alternative contact points?
- Are they fully consistent with a single electronic IP-enabled service?

These are all questions retail banks are asking, and some are answering ... and it ain't easy. But it has to start with the network being the IP network of the 21st century and not the high street bricks network of the 20th and before.

The multichannel myth (2009)

For years, I've dealt with banks talking about multichannel integration and adding new capabilities to the core traditional channel of branch operations. In the 1970s we added ATMs; the 1980s added call centres; the 1990s the internet, and now mobile.

For all those years, we merrily added these techno-capabilities as the world revolved around us because we felt we had to and because, in some cases, they saved us money.

We added ATMs because they reduced costs; we added call centres because new competitors were eating our lunch; we added the internet because we thought we could close branches; and we're adding mobile because it's the latest fad for customer service.

For all those years, we did the best we could to keep up ... but we failed.

You see, I had a realisation this week. One of those eureka moments. The realisation that multichannel does not work. It was something that we've been doing in our sleep, but it's wrong.

What we actually created is mixichannel. Mixi stands for mixed up.

We added ATMs and they've grown massively in the UK, from 10,000 in 1986 to over 60,000 today. These were typically stuck on the outside of branches and are now in car parks, pubs, casinos and anywhere else you might need cash. The ATM saved cash by increasing transactional services without the human hand involved, or not the bank's hand anyway.

The ATM, however, is not really a channel. It's an adjunct to the bank's reach. It's a cost reduction mechanism. It's a method of getting rid of a branch or adding a remote branch, but it's a transaction engine.

It's not a channel. A channel is somewhere where you can sell stuff and provide advice.

Anyone lingering at an ATM talking about a pension would either be (a) mad, or (b) annoying, as the 100 people standing behind them wanting cash will be out with the daggers.

So the ATM is not a channel as such, but call centre, internet and mobile are channels.

And the thing about the call centre, internet and mobile is that the banks have typically added these channels onto existing operations after another player has proven their success.

In the case of the call centre, First Direct was one of the first movers to make this channel work, and is the UK's leader in this area. First Direct built their bank around a remote telephone based centre, rather than adding call centre to branch operations. Therefore, the difference is that First Direct has processes designed for remote customer reach, rather than a process designed for administering customer service when the branch is closed.

In the case of the internet, Britain's leading internet bank is Smile. Smile is a bank designed for exploiting internet self-servicing, rather than adding traditional bank processes to a home-based self-service channel.

And in the case of mobile, we now have a new dedicated mobile bank, Mobank, which is soon to launch in the UK.

What's the point?

Well, my eureka moment is that the banks of the 1970s are still the banks of the 1970s.

The reason why their call centre operations ask for name and account number, and focus upon balance and transaction statements, is because they view the branch as the key contact point.

The reasons their internet services are dull and boring is because they are just automating statements online, rather than leveraging and using broadband-based social media.

And their mobile services will be the same.

This is because the technology is being added to the bank focused around branch operations, rather than using the technology to design a new bank specifically for that technology.

However, when a bank is designed around the technology, it wipes the floor of the competition. First Direct is not only Britain's largest call centre-based bank, but it's one of Britain's favourite banks. Smile is not only an internet designed bank for internet access, but also Britain's favourite bank. They are banks without branches designed for the channels of today, rather than banks with branches who added these channels onto their traditional structures.

In Japan, I recently talked about Jibun Bank and eBank. eBank has half of the internet banking market in Japan, as a bank designed for the internet. Jibun Bank has already stormed up the bank charts, as a bank designed for the mobile.

What this tells me is that it's not about banks closing down and being eaten by new competition, as all of these banks other than eBank are owned by traditional branch-based banks.

What it says is that a bank is far more likely to be successful with a new channel if they design a bank for that channel, rather than tagging on the technology as another on top of their branch operations.

Just a thought as, if true, it says that banks should really be launching new banks designed for new channels under separate brands as their future strategy, whilst making the absolute mini-

It's Banking Jim, But Not As We Know It

mum investment in the new channel with their older channel brands.

Some banks do the latter anyway, but I'm not sure whether it's by design or lethargy.

Final thought: if my business can run today for 80% of the costs it did a decade ago, thanks to broadband access and low-cost technology, why hasn't a bank passed on these savings to their customers?

UK bank branch numbers declined 11% between 2002 and 2007, and broadband means that UK banks have most customers looking after their own needs these days through self-service. Call centres have been outsourced and offshored, and ATMs have extended to cheque deposits and more.

All in all, banks should have reduced costs massively for distribution and service over the past decade ... so how come customers aren't seeing the cost reductions?

Just a thought, and one I'll come back to I'm sure.

Bank branches and next gen mobile (2010)

I spent a lot of time yesterday talking with folks about the future of money, payments and banking. The conversation got interesting in two particular areas: branches and mobile services. This is because I realised some things.

Take branches. There appears to be an evolution of branch usage from underbanked economies through emerging economies to developed economies. In the underbanked economies, the issue is often a mixture of a lack of infrastructure and investment combined with low income and low prospects. In these instances, banks don't make investments in branches as there is only going to be profitability from clients in major urban areas where there's population density, wealth and work.

As a result, these countries have had little banking prospects, availability or access, but this is changing due to the introduction of mobile wireless infrastructures.

Even so, these communities will still remain underbanked as full bank services have limited availability in rural communities.

You then move to emerging economies, and find the massive urbanisation of these economies is creating new wealth and new communities. You only have to look at the urbanisation of China, with the rural population to urban population changing from 74% to 26% in 1990 to a major switch in 2009 of 53.4% rural to 46.6% urban to realise such change. And with such change, comes branches and branch banking. China has seen a revolution in banking during their change process, and today's Chinese banks hardly reflect those of two decades ago in service and style. In this instance, mobile services range from simple to complex, and the mobile channel is everything from basic payments to full service banking depending upon which consumer segment the bank serves.

Then you look at developed economies, and the bank branch is already inbuilt to their model from the past. The branch may be an asset or liability, but the criticality is that new channels and technologies – internet and mobile internet specifically – are offering additional and alternative capabilities for these banks to reach their consumer.

This also varies by culture and language. For example, Spanish bank customers much prefer bank branch access than UK customers, who would rather call their bank than visit a branch.

So you cannot generalise too much about these services. Nevertheless, and this was my other realisation: you can also see big changes in mobile.

I'm no mobile expert but in banking, I've seen five phases of mobile channel access and usage. The first was basic payments processing and transaction services using SMS text messaging.

It's Banking Jim, But Not As We Know It

Then there were additional bank account services based upon Wireless Application Protocol, WAP. Third-generation mobile bank services offered a more multimedia-rich interaction, based upon smartphones. This was OK, but limited by the fact that you had to design your apps for each phone operating system and, in some cases, model of phone. Hence, it was very limited.

Fourth generation is where we are today, and I have talked about the killer apps offered by iPhones and Androids. The beauty of this generation is not only that we now have phones that can offer idiot-proof bank services, but apps that can be developed and deployed for mobile internet. Therefore, the design is no longer for a specific phone model or operating system, but for easy access to multimedia-rich banking services using Open APIs.

Finally, there is a next generation mobile service appearing on the horizon ... the chip-neutral device.

Today, we have EMV chips for cards, SIM chips for phones and RFID chips for contactless services. This is all going to change in the next few years as Visa, MasterCard, the GSMA and mobile operators work together to develop chip enabled services that are device-neutral.

Hence you could stick your communicating wireless payments chip into any machinery, gadget, tool or technology you want ... a telephone, a watch, a television, an iPad, a laptop, a pair of sunglasses ... anything and everything can become a wirelessly communicating, interactive payments device.

Roll on the next generation.

Banks should be cannibals (2009)

Banks need to become cannibals. Banks should launch new channels that eat their old ones alive, rather than trying to bolt these new channels onto their old bank.

Banks can only be brilliant at one channel – the branch, the call centre or the internet – and the other channels are an addendum.

This means the other channels cannot compete with specialists who build for that channel, so they fail.

Therefore, launch new dedicated bank structures for each channel, rather than trying to mix them together.

Eat your old channels alive!

But it goes beyond that. The world is changing and changing fast. When Twitter can go from unknown to mainstream within a year, you know the world is changing fast.

Equally, if I can now run a business that is 80% cheaper today because of a broadband connection, how come banks have not reduced their fees similarly?

How come, when customers are performing all the administration of their accounts through internet access, they have to pay the bank a fee for an account?

It should be, and will be, free!

Why not have a bank account funded by Google ads?

Why not offer a complete financial service including credit facilities, funded by customers accepting to receive sponsored advertisements before they see their statements?

Take this even further. What if the customer could design their banking world? This is surely possible if the customer is allowed to integrate best-of-breed widgets for each of their financial needs – savings, loans, transactions, mortgages, insurances – into each of their channels of choice – mobile, internet, telephone, branch. This way the customer can design their financial management to suit their lifestyle.

What does this mean for the traditional bank and its branch structures?

It means that the bank of the very near future will see consumers and corporates taking pieces of financial functionality from specialists who offer this functionality at very low margins in the form of widgets.

For the traditional bank, it will mean that the specialists will steal the high margin streams of business – savings, loans, mortgages, insurances – because these providers, which may well include traditional banks, will offer such financial functionality at a fraction of the cost of traditional processing rates.

This is because the new players will be offering better technology platforms at razor-thin margins, because they have no overheads of structure, are low-cost and low-staffed, and are specialised and targeted at just that functionality through that channel.

This leaves the traditional bank with a very expensive branch infrastructure as their premier channel of choice for distribution and focus. That branch will be left with transactions, because all the sexy stuff will be taken by these new, razor-thin margin players, who design for their electronic channels of choice.

In other words, the branch is processing commodity transactions for no margin with limited ability to upscale to more profitable business.

Oh dear.

Another reason why traditional banks need to rethink their economics, structures and approach before their business will be disrupted beyond recognition.

Branch or internet? A clear winner! (2008)

I have posed the question branch or internet, and made it an extreme choice. Everyone says you would never have such a stark choice, but there was reason in my madness. And the reason is that we are caught in a wave of the second internet boom, and are we in danger of repeating the mistakes of the past?

Just think for a second and look back.

A decade ago, we were in the grip of the first internet boom, where we all invested in internet banking and online self-service. The result was that everyone felt that branches were redundant. People weren't going to branches for advice or sales. They were just transaction centres, so let's close them all down. And many did.

(...)

Now, in 2008, everyone is riding a new technology wave: m-networking or m-net for short.

m-net is all about Web 2.0 and mobile communications. But I wonder whether we are in danger of repeating our mistakes of the last decade by focusing upon m-net at the expense of branches.

(...)

Here's my view.

We are caught up in another technology rollercoaster, wrapped up in social networking, Web 2.0 and mobile banking and payments. We have no idea whether our investments in these services will ever provide a return, or are even appropriate to our customers, but feel we have to try out services in this space as they might just be transformational, or even fundamental, to future growth.

The branch is still languishing as something we are not sure we need long term, and we are trying to rationalise them to turn them into sales centres with automated transactions, whilst closing the smaller ones or turning them into self-service lobbies.

We are using customer demographics to try to deliver the services customers want through the channels they choose. Segment customers through channels of their choice, which naturally leads to many thinking mature customers want branches whilst young customers want self-service m-net systems.

All very laudable. All complete clap-trap.

For a start, you cannot use demographics as a sign of anything anymore. (...) The demographics of m-net is no longer kids.

It's Banking Jim, But Not As We Know It

It's mums and dads, grandmas and grandpas, so stop thinking of customers as segments with clear attributes. It is more a
case of groups of people who can be psychologically profiled to
have preferences for how they are dealt with through different
delivery capabilities. As a result, you need to know more about
the psychological preferences of these groups, rather than their
demographics. I'm not saying demographics are unimportant,
but that psychographics are far more important today.

Now to the point: what are you going to do with that $10
million investment?

If it were such a stark choice today, I'd stick it in branches.

There, I've said it. Heathen.

Why? Because the majority of banks will not see a near-term
ROI m-net investments as there are few banks offering these services and, of the ones that are, you may not find them to be in your
space. If they are in your space as a direct competitor, then take
notice and think about it.

There are a few banks using m-net for innovation and differentiation, and a few creating business models that will deliver ROI
long-term. When they do, you can follow them. That's the point –
when it works, follow it and most customers will not change their
bank for a wiki, widget or mobile service. If and when they do,
then follow it fast as a fast follower.

More importantly, as proven by the recent crisis, customers
want a physical place to go when they're nervous if, for no other
reason, than seeking assurance. If the internet site has a blip these
days or freezes for 10 seconds, they think the bank has gone bank-
rupt. By having branches, you're far more reassuring. And if those
branches look and feel nice, even better.

Finally, the m-net area is going to make a difference, but whilst
customers seek to re-establish trust with banks, relationships
need to be close, not remote. So build relationships through
strong branch services.

There. That's the heathen bit out of the way.

Now, if you do happen to have $10 million spare after doing what you need to do with the branches then yes, please, stick it into m-net projects as this will secure your future. This is because the banks that come out of the next few years the strongest, will be those that deliver fantastic branch relationships enhanced by m-net capabilities that are exceptional.

For the few banks that do that today – and there are a few – this is their opportunity to wipe out competition and, if you are competing with the few that I'm thinking about, then you better get in there quick as they are eating your lunch.

I'm watching that space.

Bank channel strategies are fundamentally flawed (2007)

For half a millennium, retail banks have worked on the basis of physical distribution. For half a century, that model has been challenged to move towards electronic distribution. At the end of the first decade of the new millennium, we have finally reached the point where electronic distribution has matured, works and is proven. Unfortunately, most retail banks are stuck in the 20th century. It's time for retail banks to turn their model on its head and focus upon electronic platforms where physical distribution is the cream on the cake, rather than the other way around.

(...)

Retail banks have a historically strong branch network. Each new channel is added as an extra layer on the foundation of the branch distribution cake. Branch networks are the foundations – electronic distribution is the cream on the cake.

This is why retail banks talk about multichannel strategies where they try to integrate their call centre channel with their internet channel; they attempt to deliver mobile banking interop-

It's Banking Jim, But Not As We Know It

erable with the call centre channel; they mess about with CRM to ensure consistency across branch and internet channels.

My problem is this: banks only have one channel.

They do not have multi-channels, call centre channels, internet channels, mobile channels and so forth. They just have an electronic channel that underscores and provides the foundation for all end points: mobile, telephone, internet and branch.

The electronic channel is based upon internet protocol (IP) technologies, as is the branch as it happens. And this is the big change. Just as I referenced that mobile telephony is wrong as it should be IP telephony, banks should stop thinking of channels and just recognise that they are IP-enabled. Call centre, ATMs, branch, internet, mobile ... everything is IP-enabled.

Thinking this way then demonstrates the fundamental flaw in retail banking today, because many banks still have everything built in layers of complexity and legacy.

The ATM, call centre and internet channels were all built as layers of cake created when the physical branch was the foundation. The electronic channels were built as ancilliary to the core branch channel. That is why they were often separated and have this chasm of non-integration between each other, as banks were built on a physical distribution model where electronics were layered on top.

However, today, and certainly tomorrow, the population has moved to a world where the majority are digital natives. As the digital generation grows up and matures, and as the world becomes one populated by digital natives, what role will there be for banks that have been built upon the basis of a physical distribution model with electronics layered on top?

It's time to turn this on its head. It's time to think about banking as an electronic structure. It's time to bite the bullet and admit that retail banking is not a physical distribution structure with electronic channels on top, but an electronic distribution structure with electronic and physical channels on top.

How does that change thinking?

It would mean wiping the slate clean and starting afresh.

How would we build today's bank if IP-networking is its foundation; and call centre, internet, mobile and the branch are just the cream of the cake on top? Where would you build branches, and how would you build them, if the branches are ancillary and perfunctory to the electronic foundations? Who would you employ, and how would you employ them, if the core differentiation of the bank is its IP base rather than its branch structure?

The fact is, that any bank that launched today as a green field operation would think this way and, with the right leadership and implementation, it would thrash the weak competition that exists in most markets which are based upon legacy structures and legacy thinking.

Start thinking about the bank being an IP network at its core, with layers of distribution on top and branch as the cream on the cake.

It's time for change.

Chapter 5 The mobile future of banking

Introduction

In 2003, I predicted that mobile telephones would revolution-ise bank services. Bearing in mind that this was just after most banks had lost a fortune playing around with mobiles using WAP applications, most folks laughed. On the other hand, this predic-tion was based upon the emergent and nascent market for smart-phones and 3G services. A few years later and banks and telecoms firms are fighting tooth and nail to win the mobile financial space. This has resulted in a sudden flourish of bank and mobile innova-tions such as M-PESA in Kenya, a Vodafone success, and Jibun Bank in Japan, a mobile-only bank partnership between KDDI and Bank of Tokyo Mitsubishi. It is now obvious that mobile internet-based banking is the biggest channel development for the next decade. How this might play out is discussed below.

The mobile financial future (2009)

There are loads of discussions about mobile financial services right now, not least at the Financial Services Club. We recently held three meetings: the first in Austria in April; then in London in May; and finally in Dublin in June, and all about mobile finan-cial services.

The common theme amongst all three meetings is that mobile banking and financial services is BIG news, with speakers includ-ing Volksbank, Royal Bank of Scotland, Monitise, MoBank, Cap Gemini, S1, IND and Edgar Dunn.

So here's a rapid summary of what folks said.

First, Martin-Hannes Giesswein, Head of Retail for Nokia Alps & Southeast Europe, presented Nokia's core view that kids are being introduced to mobile young and, with most of the world now able to access mobiles, you would be silly to ignore this space.

This was corroborated by Roy Vella, who heads up mobile for Royal Bank of Scotland, who pointed out that half the planet now has access to mobiles. A point that was stressed by Samee Zafar, Director with Edgar Dunn & Co. There are more mobiles being bought per second than babies being born!

József Nyíri, Chief Technology Officer with IND Group, made the point that mobile is this major channel because it is easier than using a PC, whilst Richard Johnson, Chief Strategy Officer with Monitise, stressed that it is a critical channel for getting rid of nuisance calls, such as those that are just balance checking.

All of these firms, banks, infrastructure and solutions providers believe the same thing: if you're not into mobile yet, you're going to be dead meat.

This was truly illustrated by Steve Townend, Chief Executive Officer with MoBank, who discussed what happened when they started a pre-release programme for their banking service on the iPhone. Steve's point was that the MoBank iPhone app was launched in beta mode and, as a result of being listed as a half-decent financial app on the Apple App download listings, it shot up from no downloads to 3,000 in a day.

How do you scale to handle that sudden viral impact of being noticed? Cloud computing I guess, as this was similar to the issues Animoto experienced last year.

Animoto is a little-known service that makes it really easy for people to create videos with their own photos or their own music. Last year, they became a classic case study in cloud computing because they suddenly went from zero to hero over one weekend.
(...)

In summary, I know this combines a lot of different points, but they are all related:

- Mobile technologies are transforming banking services globally;
- From simple text payments to full banking services, there are many examples of this transformation;
- The challenge is how to keep up with the speed of innovation and the speed of viral change; and
- When a mention on iPhone apps shifts MoBank from 50 downloads a day to 3,000, how do you keep up?
- Similarly, viral networking through other social media can result in a similar upclick in hours (think of Susan Boyle going from nothing to 200 million video views in only a month!); and so
- Cloud computing and the Animoto story maybe show the way, where you can upscale by buying server space on demand.

Our world is one where mobile social networking enables viral financial apps to transform an unknown bank into a dominant player in hours.

The world is changing ... are you keeping up?

Mobile money (2009)

Just found a few numbers on mobile money users and thought it worth sharing:

- The market for mobile applications, or apps, will become "as big as the internet", peaking at 10 million apps in 2020 according to Symbian.
- CGAP produced a recent survey on financial access and found that there are 6.2 billion bank accounts worldwide – more than one for every person on the planet – except that 70% of adults in developing countries do not use formal financial services, or are unbanked, compared to 20% of those in developed countries.

- Of the 139 countries that CGAP surveyed, only 40 reported that they encourage or mandate government transfers through the banking system; 14 of these are high-income countries and 10 countries in Latin America. Few countries in other regions are promoting such transfers.
- The survey predicts that the mobile payments market could be worth as much as £365 billion by 2013, with 110 million users in Europe alone by 2014.
- By the year 2012 CGAP and GSMA estimate there will be 1.7 billion people with a mobile phone but not a bank account and as many as 364 million unbanked people could be reached by agent-networked banking through mobile phones.
- CGAP estimates that mobile financial services to poor people in emerging economies will increase from nothing to $5 billion in 2012.
- 40% of Kenyan households have used M-PESA as of late 2008.
- 41% of Filipino mobile money users were able to set up a mobile money account in five minutes or less.
- Electronic payments deliver cost savings of at least 1% of a country's GDP when compared to paper, according to Visa.
- Monitise, the mobile money network, has just signed up their millionth customer and are processing 25 million transactions per annum.

Is mobile banking the future or a waste of money? (2008)

This week was spent in various meetings and dialogues, one of which was all about mobile payments and mobile banking. Now,

It's Banking Jim, But Not As We Know It

I've seen a lot about mobile banking and payments in the last couple of years, and had a moment to reflect on experiences.

In particular I was struck by the fact that, in 2003, I asked a group of American bankers: "When will mobile be an effective channel for payments and banking?" The answer came back unanimously as at least five years away, and probably 10.

Five years later and mobile is ubiquitous and pervasive.

During my reflections, I also realised how diverse the range of mobile finance applications are today.

At the entry level are text messaging payment services, such as Smart Money and GCash in the Philippines. Smart has over 33 million subscribers, more than 7 million of whom are in the Smart Money system. Globe Telecom has around 1.5 million users of the GCash service.

Then, upscale, are services such as the 'Osaifu Keitai' (mobile wallet) in Japan, which allows users to integrate RFID with mobile and credit card to create a fully functional mobile payments service.

NTT DoCoMo has over 25 million 'Osaifu Keitai' (mobile wallet) phones in issue with over 310,000 acceptance points. NTT DoCoMo also offers the 'iD' credit card service for its phone owners which has round 4.5 million users since its launch in December 2005 and more than 250,000 terminals in retailers, which include petrol stations, taxis and convenience stores. This has now been emulated by others, such as O2 with Visa in London.

Then there's fuller mobile banking, such as Bank of America. Bank of America launched mobile banking in May 2007 and by July 2008 reached over a million customers, with 10,000 registering a mobile banking session every hour! Most of them use the service to view account balances and review transactions.

Finally, there's the Web 2.0 rich style mobile applications rolled out by BBVA this summer with *Tú Cuentas* (You Count).

In this instance, you not only have basic payments and banking services, but full wiki style plug and play applications, with budgeting, alerts, aggregation and more.

From something that wasn't even being considered seriously by most banks five years ago, mobile today is a critical channel for banking ...

... or is it?

October 2008 – how many people use mobile banking in your country? Here in the UK, I only know of a few examples and, according to IBM, very few want it. In a survey issued this month, IBM found that half of the general populous would substitute their Internet usage on a PC for a mobile device. In particular, travel, news and information services are all expected to increase significantly in popularity and usage. However, the survey also found that consumers still prefer to execute services such as banking and stock trading on a PC rather than on a mobile.

What's the truth?

My own view? People don't know what they want till they have it. Once they realise what they can do with instant balance checks at point of sale and pay with the wave of the phone, they'll start using mobile banking and IBM's report just reflects that lack of availability of mobile financial services.

Mobile really is the future of banking (2008)

I have often said that tracking the future is normally demonstrated by tracking children's behaviours. Kids are excited about the future. They are desperately keen to rush headlong into the next week, month and year. As a result of this excitement about going forwards, many of the future trends are activated by children first. They then educate the adults in how things work. After

It's Banking Jim, But Not As We Know It

all, we grown-ups are far more concerned about no-one moving our cheese than trying to be older before our time.

In fact, most adults are running away from the future: we don't like change, we want things to be routine and stable. Kids want things to be unpredictable and unstable. So, track children's behaviours to see the future.

Kids were the first into chatrooms, with their own language, such as lol and pos*. Then they started txt msg so m&d hd 2 rd bks 2 c wt thy wr syg**. Now they use emoticons for everything :P

So I'm always interested to read surveys of teen and children's habits as I think it will tell me a lot about the future of channels, branding, engagement and learning how to market to the next generation customer. It also helps to see what our adult consumers might be being taught by their children shortly.

The reason for mentioning all of this is that Habbo has just produced a fascinating survey of kids. If you are not aware, Habbo is a child-oriented virtual world; a bit like a Second Life or Entropia for tweenies. To gain an insight into what those tweens (11-18 years old) think, Habbo asked 58,480 people aged between 11 and 18 in over 31 countries across Europe, America and Latin America about their internet habits during October and November 2007.

The results are fascinating, and build on their first survey back in 2006.

- ◆ 76% of tweens use instant messaging as their main method of staying in touch with friends online;
- ◆ 72% have email accounts, but it is being used less and less;
- ◆ Email usage is primarily just for official communications with parents and employers;
- ◆ 71% of tweens listen to music on their mobile, compared to only 38% in 2006;

- 70% use their mobiles to take photos and videos, compared to 59% in 2006;
- 64% play games via the mobile, up from 50% in 2006;
- Surfing the net, emailing and sending instant messages via mobile is commonly used by over a quarter of teens;
- 40% of teenagers do not view social networks as an important part of their communication experience.

I've been aware of the declining email usage being replaced with text and IM, but the idea of not finding Bebo, Facebook and such like of importance surprised me. But then it may be explained by the fact that non-English speaking social network sites are still lacking, and non-English speaking kids do not want to use English-speaking social sites. This means that more local language sites will rise in importance and is why sites such as Vostu, a Facebook in Spanish and Portuguese, are of note.

Meanwhile, banks should think about IM and mobile more in this context. Yes, banks are doing lots of mobile payments and mobile banking trials and roll-outs, but using this as a sales channel rather than a services channel appears to be seriously underused and misunderstood today.

However, within a few months or years, mum and dad will be learning these technologies to keep in touch with little Johnny. Therefore, mobile communications will be possibly the most critical sales and services channel of the future, rather than just a pilot or experiment.

Now you may think that this is the opposite of something I said a while ago, about mobile being rubbish. But this commentary was about mobile being rubbish as things converge towards VOIP, and that point still holds true.

So banking of the near future will be mobile VOIP with IM, and a whole lot more and, interestingly, social networking is already moving to mobiles. For example, according to this description of a brand new, not yet released or named, mobile-based social networking tool: "it shows you everyone around you who has it installed on an iPhone. Users can scroll through nearby users, and set filters for men, women or age ranges. If you find someone interesting you can pull up their profile and ping them. If they respond you can start a chat, on the phone or in person."

Maybe the future is here already.

Is your bank ready to be an MVBO? (2008)

I spent yesterday with a group of Japanese bankers discussing the future of banking. Actually, I say 'discussing' but Japanese bankers are very polite and so there were very few questions. Therefore, I spent yesterday with a group of Japanese bankers telling them about the future of banking.

All of this was with simultaneous translation which is never an easy experience for me or for them, as you crack a joke and it gets a laugh five minutes later. Then you wonder why everyone's laughing and whether it was at your joke or something the translator said.

Anyways, in the afternoon some friends of mine joined us, and I was particularly intrigued to hear the plans of Roy Vella, who heads up mobile banking for Royal Bank of Scotland.

For over a year now, the 'hot' topic at all the places I visit has been mobile banking. Thus far, many of my favourite stories of mobile finance tend to come from Asia, such as the mobile wallet Edy in Japan run by NTT DoCoMo. I also like the experience of Bank of America, which has gained over a million customers since launching their mobile banking last year.

But Roy had a slightly different story, and talked about M-PESA for a while. I thought that was strange, as M-PESA is Vodafone's implementation of mobile money transfers between folks in Kenya (through their subsidiary Safaricom), and the last time I heard about M-PESA was the announcement of Vodafone's joint venture with Citi to roll this out worldwide. So why would Roy talk about this as his launchpad when he's with Royal Bank of Scotland?

Well, let's tell it as Roy tells it.

Vodafone was asked to set up M-PESA by the Kenyan government, and launched the service in March 2007 as a joint venture, 40% owned by Vodafone Kenya and 60% by the government, which they reduced to 35% through a privatisation sale in June.

The actual service provides a simple way to move money between people using mobile messaging, but it has revolutionised the country. This is because most people in Kenya were unbanked, so they either had cash or nothing. No credit and debit cards, cheques or other ways of paying.

Now, with the mobile telephone as the core value exchange mechanism, it has changed everything. As one farmer is quoted in CGAP, "I can just walk from my shamba (farm) and get money. I don't have to spend and go into town. If the agent does not have cash today, then I will come back tomorrow. It is cheaper to wait." And now, he doesn't even have to wait for the agent as M-PESA is available through Pesapoint ATMs.

As Roy puts it, this means that you have African and other emerging economies leapfrogging developed economies as: (a) they have jumped to telecommunications without ever laying landlines; and (b) they have jumped to electronic payments without ever having cheques or cards. No legacy infrastructures involved.

Originally, Vodafone and the government estimated they would gain about 200,000 users in the first year. By the end of year one, they had achieved 10 times that number with over 2 million users, combined with over 200,000 people signing up every month. With only 4 million people with bank accounts in Kenya, this means that within a couple of years, Vodafone have accidentally become the largest bank in Kenya.

107

To put this in context, M-PESA's monthly volume of transactions in Kenya alone is more than the largest money transfer operator, Western Union, transfers globally.

The thing is, Vodafone never wanted to become Kenya's biggest bank, and here's where the Royal Bank of Scotland (RBS) strategy steps in. RBS is focusing upon being the manufacturer of payments processing for telcos as an MVBO, a Mobile Virtual Banking Operator. Roy likened this to an MVNO, a Mobile Virtual Network Operator, where mobile firms manufacturer call processing that can be 'white-labelled' by others. For example, O2 is the call processor for Virgin Mobile calls. So RBS will do the same for payments. O2, Orange, T-Mobile, Hutchinson ... whoever wants to process payments in the M-PESA-style roll-out can do so by just selecting their preferred MVBO for each country. And with 60% of the world unbanked, but many with access to a mobile phone, that's a huge untapped market.

Interesting. I wonder how many MVBOs there will be in the world by 2010?

Africa's mobile financial revolution (2009)

I know that the theme of mobile banking is appearing a lot at the moment, but it is hot, hot, hot! A bit like Africa, and this is the story of a great success in Africa. And no, it's not M-PESA, although that one's a goodie too. This one's ABSA Bank in South Africa.

ABSA launched mobile payment services back in 2000 and saw a gradual growth in usage, with a near enough doubling of users year-on-year to reach over one million customers today.

Over half of these customers use mobile banking for balance checking, but buying prepaid airtime and looking at mini-statements are also very popular. The service not only offers simple

SMS payment services, but goes a step further by tapping into the functionality of USSD.

USSD allows more functionally rich processes and services to a standard GSM telephone and therefore balance checks and beyond, and is the method by which ABSA Bank has built an affinity for the mobile handset as a financial tool.

Not only is it used for customers to make simple transactions therefore, but the service also offers alerts as an early warning system for fraud. This means that for every payment on debit or credit card, customers can set alerts to their telephone to reduce fraudulent activity. You can also parameterise those alerts, based upon size of transaction or location.

Here's Christo Vrey, Managing Executive, Digital Channels for ABSA Bank discussing the service, who made it clear that:
- (a) Moving the channel from a simple transaction to a useful service for anti-fraud management, customers will pay for the additional services; and
- (b) Moving the channel from a simple transactional system to a mobile financial channel increases the opportunity to grow market.

This is made clear in the chart below:

It's Banking Jim, But Not As We Know It

Mobile banking adoption has grown very rapidly in the past five years (South Africa)

Historical Perspective & Projection until end of 2010*			
Year	Customers	Transaction Volume	Transaction Value
2001	+- 9 500	+- 410k	+- R89m
2003	+- 47 000	+- 2,4 mil pa	+- R392mil pa
2009	+- 2.4m (120 000 pm)	+- 21mil pm/252mil pa	+- R16bn pa
2010	+- 5m	+- 63mil pm/630 mil pa	+- R40bn pa $4.0bn @ R10
Mobile Channel figures including Messaging			
Year	Customers	SMS Transaction Volume	Transaction Value
2009	+- 12m (450 000 pm)	+- 250mil pm/3.5 bil pa	N/A
2010	+-15m	+- 500mil pm/7 bil pa	N/A

What this shows is that they had forecast the market size to be about 5 million people based upon simple SMS payments but, by adding SMS alerts and USSD the market size triples.

The reason for this is the bank extends the range and breadth of mobile services, to leverage this as a channel rather than as an ancillary. For example, the bank makes it mandatory to use the mobile as a kind of Xiring terminal, where every online payment is authorised through a one time password (OTP) via an SMS text message.

All sorts of other information is provided through the mobile including notice of payment to beneficiaries, account activity notifications relating to ATM withdrawals and debit order payments, and more. In other words, the bank has tried to create an affinity for customers with their mobile bank as their primary transaction and verification tool.

One of the biggest pieces of their service is a demonstration, however.

A demonstration? Sure. How many people use an ATM if no-one shows them how? How many people use self-service internet, if no-one shows them how? And how many people use mobile channels, if no-one shows them how?

Now you may think this is not important, but the most important aspect of ABSA's experience is that customers swarmed to the service after they rolled out a sales force. This sales force demonstrated the service to customers as they went to ATMs across South Africa, and were easily identifiable as they were wearing the bank's bright red livery.

The fact that people took the time to explain the service explains the blip you see in ABSA's customers between 2007 and 2009. It also shows the reason for the interest in this service, in that you are looking at a country where geography is a barrier to payments. Getting money from A to B has been traditionally tough, with bus drivers and taxi's being the only way to normally move money around in an insecure and unreliable way.

In fact, you can combine the story of ABSA, which is really getting into the banked population, with the story of M-PESA which is driving into the unbanked population, and the stories provide a common theme.

First, geography is a key factor. The fact that Africa lacked the infrastructure for some of the payments and other processes we are used to means that the wireless banking capabilities of mobile make it a key.

And the second factor speaks for itself: mobility. The fact that mobile communications are now in play, overcomes the need for physical movements of the days of old. And the days of old to which I refer are less than five years ago.

For example, I was lucky enough to hear Olga Morawczynksi of CGAP talk about M-PESA last week, at the excellent Digital Money Forum. Olga made it clear that the reason for the rapid take-up of M-PESA is twofold.

It's Banking Jim, But Not As We Know It

First, men naturally migrate to Nairobi for work, leaving wives and family in rural villages who need money to buy essentials such as wheat, maize and more. Many of those in the rural communities depend upon these remittances for anything from half to all of their income. The fact the migrant worker can now instantaneously get the money home without having to leave the city for days, or pay someone a large commission to move funds, is the reason why it works with the typical user making six M-PESA transactions per month in a mixture of remittances and savings.

The second reason was the political unrest in Kenya during the recent elections, which meant saving with a 'trusted' provider such as M-PESA, which is run by a South African, became more trusted than saving with a Kenyan Bank, especially as some of those banks went bust (sounds familiar?).

By January 2009, M-PESA had 5.5 million users out of Safaricom's 13 million subscribers representing a third of Kenya's 36 million population. Those M-PESA users are making 160,000 person-to-person payments every day through a network of M-PESA agents, each of whom processes around 90 transactions a day earning US$5 in commissions. US$5 a day in Kenya is a good rate of earnings when the average casual labourer only makes $1 a day.

All in all, the rapid take-up of a new technology, accessible to all through mobile GSM communications in a mixture of SMS and USSD is proving to be a massive success in several African communities.

It will be nice when we can get it here!

Britain's first mobile bank (2009)

I was pleased to hear about the progress of MoBank, the UK's first mobile-only bank, which launches in May. It's not a fully fledged bank yet, like Jibun Bank, as it's starting out as a convenient way to buy things through an iPhone and designed for young adults. So it doesn't have all the transactional capabilities of a normal banking service but it will, as MoBank plans to offer a savings account, P2P payments, account aggregation, bill payments and a virtual prepaid card over time.

Steve Townend, MoBank's CEO and co-founder, presented the firm's plans at a conference with me last week. Steve and fellow co-founder of MoBank, Dominic Keen, both worked together at Egg. Strangely enough, many of the founders of Zopa also worked at Egg, which may be indicative of where to look for these entrepreneurs of new models of finance. Steve was also head of lending at First Direct, so he knows a bit about telephone banking, internet banking and disruptive banking innovation.

Now, I've heard Steve talk about MoBank's plans before but it is now ready to launch, having secured a further $1 million in funds in January, so here's the low-down.

MoBank is a new mobile service that allows customers to buy and pay for goods wherever and whenever they want. By working with the customers' existing account it is a convenient and secure way to make day-to-day transactions and administer personal finances from a mobile phone or any Internet connected device.

MoBank works on the iPhone and iPhone touch and is primarily targeted for students and young adults, with 100,000 of them expected to sign up in the first year. I particularly like the MoBank interface which is a very easy-to-use and attractive iPhone applet that makes buying convenience plays – such as cinema tickets, flowers, mobile top-ups and similar goods and services – a breeze.

From launch, MoBank will offer cinema tickets, clothes, music, books, train tickets, flowers, gifts and takeaways on the service. A typical example of the services concepts is that people will use MoBank when they are on their way out, for example, and they realise they have forgotten their Mum's birthday or whatever.

In this case, they can send her flowers just by ordering, buying and paying for them via MoBank on their mobile phone. To do this, the user simply downloads the MoBank application, regis-

It's Banking Jim, But Not As We Know It

ter their credit or debit card which gives them a secure MoBank PIN. The PIN can then pay for any services through the MoBank service.

This is a core focal point for MoBank, which works with affiliate partners and earns a percentage of each sale as their revenue model. For example, the flower firm Interflora gives MoBank 8% of any sale as a fee for distribution through their channel. This fee payment from affiliates may be a far better route to follow than interchange fees, and is representative once again of another disruptive model of finance.

Shortly after launch, the service will also add further money management applications to pay bills and IOUs, and transfer money between accounts, as well as features such as a birthday and special dates reminder alert, and a budget tracker to help keep track of spending.

What particularly intrigued me is that MoBank has had hardly any coverage to date, but the 35 articles that have featured the firm generated over 10 million visitors to their message, many of them American.

Obviously there's a lot of interest in mobile banking out there!

Jibun Bank: a mobile-only bank (2009)

I've talked about UMPay, a JV between Unionpay and China Mobile, as well as eBank, an internet bank leader in Japan now owned by an etailer, Rakuten Group. This leads nicely into what is probably the most innovative bank I've seen so far: Jibun Bank, a Japanese bank which translates into 'my bank' in English.

Why is Jibun Bank an innovation? Because it is designed purely and simply for mobile telephone access.

Jibun Bank was launched in July 2008 by the Bank of Tokyo-Mitsubishi UFJ (BTMU) and KDDI, the Japanese telecommunications carrier. Jibun Bank now has around 400,000 customers. That may not seem like many, but it's not bad for a mobile-only bank. In fact, it's better than not bad when you think the bank is only six months old.

The aim is that, through KDDI's mobile telephone stores and BTMU's branches, you get full service access via 24-7 telephony. The 24-hour bank is also designed for mobile phone subscribers of KDDI's au mobile phone service, allowing au users to pay for goods and services they purchase with their mobile handsets and making money transfers between au subscribers as easy as just entering the receiver's telephone number and the amount of money to be transferred into the handset.

Meanwhile, to deposit or withdraw cash, customers can use BTMU's ATMs or those of Seven Bank and the Japan Post Bank.

And if you thought Jibun Bank's 5% market share was aggressive then that's just the start, as the bank has announced aggressive targets of 2.4 million accounts with deposits totalling ¥1 trillion (US$10 billion) by April 2010, rising to 3.4 million accounts and ¥1.5 trillion (UD$25 billion) the year after. That would represent over half the online market for banking.

And this is not just important to BTMU but also to KDDI, as they compete with NTT DoCoMo and Softbank to find new customers and diversify.

This means that the model of this bank is different to traditional deposit takers and lenders, as Jibun Bank expect to generate half their income from fees and the other half from investments on deposits. This places the business model closer to the 7-Eleven convenience store-style banking of Seven Bank.

Between telco banks (UMPay and Jibun Bank) and retailer banks (Seven Bank), along with eBank being owned by an etailer (Rakuten), the cross-industry partnerships and joint ventures we are likely to see in banking grow by the day.

(...)

It's Banking Jim, But Not As We Know It

Mobile payments in China (2009)

Researchers estimate that there were only 83.5 million online payment users in China in 2006, due to the lack of access to payment cards. Admittedly, Tencent with the QQ coin has enabled more payments outside the banking system, but the lack of access to e-payments has been an inhibitor to the democratisation of commerce in China.

However, this is changing and changing fast with UMPay, a Joint Venture between Unionpay and China Mobile, targeting this space through mobile services.

According to UMPay, e- and m- payment users will exceed 500 million people next year and there are already 100 million m-payment users under the UMPay scheme. That's more than the total number of online payment users only two years ago.

UMPay launched in 2003 and provides China Mobile users with a comprehensive mobile payment platform and mobile payment system provide mobile wallets, financial message services, top-ups and mobile ticketing.

However, where they are going to gain the greatest growth is from rural farmers. This is the strategy of UMPay today – to saturate the rural locations with UMPay access – and will take the 100 million users through the half a billion number in the very near future, according to UMPay CEO Bin Zhang.

Mobile finance is fast demonstrating its power in countries that are using such technologies to leapfrog established financial infrastructures. In China's case, this is a sophisticated mobile financial service from billing and payments to utilities and transportation. In other words, a comprehensive use of mobile for banking and financial services.

We could learn a thing or two.

Chapter 6 Changing customer relationships

Introduction

Throughout my work with banks, there has been this age-old dialogue about customers. It started with customer service, became customer relationship management, and is now all about the customer experience. The thing is that most other digital businesses no longer have customers, but communities. Communities are based around a circle of folks who relate to you via your banking platform. Communities are all about analysing the information of those folks to service them better. For example, analysing all the data about what people are transacting, budgeting, saving and investing to make more informed recommendations to each individual based upon the habits and lifestyles of people like them. That's what Amazon does with books, Apple does with music and Facebook does with friends. So banks need to rethink their customer relationships and start thinking about their customers as participants on their banking platform. After all, the banks that will succeed tomorrow will be those that use the data their participants share with them about their finances in the most intelligent fashion. Now, there's a challenge.

Who owns the customer? (2009)

It is unbelievable how many times I hear the cry 'Who owns the customer?' being raised by bankers, particularly during discussions about mobile telephony. Their concern is that the mobile carriers are trying to take over the customer relationship, with the result that the bank becomes a back-end commodity.

It's not just confined to mobile telephony however, as the question is raised whenever banks talk about 'partnerships' with non-banks. Being a manufacturer of banking products to a retail partner, a telco, an airline or any other business causes the bank to worry about what it means to their trust, relationship and ability to cross-sell to the end target: the customer.

Who owns the customer? Well, I've got news for you.

No-one owns the customer. The customer owns you.

The idea of 'owning' the customer is antiquated 1990s terminology, and those who use this terminology haven't woken up to the world we live in today. Today's world is one of social media and social networking.

Why don't they get it? Why can't they wake up?

Y'know what, I'm surprised they don't talk about how they split their customers into key demographics of work, age, sex, ethnicity, address and so on and so forth.

Oh, shucks. They still do.

I mean one of the guys I've been speaking to told me about how they understood all the discussions I have about internet guff, but it's just for the 18-24 student demographic isn't it?

NNNNNOOOOOOOOOOO!

And this wasn't some backwater bank in Outer Hicksville, Deadstown. No, this is a bank in one of the most technologically advanced countries of Asia. Talking about customer ownership and using old-style demographic models is just so wrong that I cannot believe this bank still exists.

So here's how it is.

There is no customer ownership, except for those customers who want to be 'owned'. These tend to be the customers who don't care. They don't see banks as having differential attributes because they believe all banks are the same. They won't change banks and just stay with you because they're too lazy, fed-up or disillusioned to change.

There are other customers who 'own' you, because you earn their loyalty and trust. They own you because they want to be with you, they enjoy their relationship with you, they see you as being an operator in their interest that suits their lifestyle and so they give you their business. In giving you their business, loyalty and trust, they expect to 'own' a relationship with you, not the other way around.

Then there are customers who seek to own the very best deal they can get, and jump around faster than Paris Hilton can find a new handbag. These guys 'own' the rates, and they don't want relationships or dialogue, they just want to get the best out of their finances. These are the folks migrating to Mint and Wesabe and other financial planning and modelling tools.

These groups of customers don't have singular attributes or homogeny of demographics.

Some are young and some are old. Some of them ignore technology channels and prefer the branch and human touch, whilst some are highly socially networked and expect to have a personalised touch through their Facebook or Twitter channel. Some live near a branch and enjoy the convenience of walking past every day with access when needed, while others have exactly the same age, locality and profile but they loathe the branch and do everything via their mobile.

There is no predictability, homogeny, ownership or relationship with any of these individuals. Just people who have financial needs who give you their business, relationship, loyalty, and even trust, as long as you earn it, keep earning it, and fit their lifestyle for the 21st century way they live.

So please stop talking about customer ownership and demographics. If you do that, you're living in the 20th century and 2010 is just a few months away.

So get with the programme.

Does customer service in banking matter? (2009)

When talking with bankers, they refer to banking as a 'utility.

It's just something that's there, like gas and electricity. It's not valuable or differentiated and no-one wakes up wondering how their payment will take place. That's why it's not priced or serviced as something of value, but just thrown out there and use it or don't, we don't care.

I say this because customers don't switch banks because they see it as just a utility, and bankers know this so they don't try to compete on customer service as they can make money regardless.

Even though it's easy to change bank accounts and the European commission is making it even easier, banks know customers can't be bothered changing because they think they're all as bad as each other.

For example, Santander took over Abbey and now Abbey gets awful customer reviews. If you go by the surveys, Abbey is the worst bank in Britain for customer service. And yet their actual customer numbers show a massive spike in customer growth. If it's known to be the worst bank in Britain for service, how come its business is growing?

Because customers don't care. Abbey offers better loan and savings rates, and customer flock to the bank.

Meanwhile, the Co-operative Bank is a lovely, cuddly bank. They're known to be eco-friendly and nice. If you call them, their customer service and call centre staff are fantastic. Nothing is offshore and it's all very personality driven and friendly. Their internet site, Smile, is regularly voted as the best in Britain and their overall bank service comes top of most people's lists.

But have they gained significant market share? No. They haven't bought customers with good rates and so the customers have not followed.

It's Banking Jim, But Not As We Know It

So banks don't need to care a jot about good customer service because it makes not a jot of difference. I mean, Wachovia was known as the best bank in America for customer satisfaction, according to the American customer satisfaction index, and look what happened to them (bust, if you didn't notice).

Added to which good service costs, and banks don't want that overhead. So do everything as cheaply as possible, don't bother giving good service and just ensure your utility works. Like gas and electricity, just make sure it works and be the lowest cost provider.

Then a little bird starts tweeting in my head: what if we made our bank the best it could possibly be? What if we broke this utility mould and focused upon being exceptional? What if we got customers to pay an annual fee, and then told them they would get the best of everything? What if we bundled all the bells and whistles on the account, and gave them birthday cards and Christmas gifts? What if we met with them once a year for a chat, called them with reminders of key things happening with their account, alerted them to better interest rates and deals whenever we released a new product ....

The what ifs are endless but, you know what, all of the above are available, have been tried and, you know what, the customers didn't care. They didn't come, they didn't pay, they didn't want it. Customers just want utility banking and bankers have become meshed in providing just a basic banking service.

Can this mutual apathy ever be broken, I wonder?

The schizophrenic bank (2009)

There are really conflicting needs in banking today, which are hard to reconcile. The result is that many banks are suffering from a form of schizophrenia where they want to be two organisations in one. The first organisation is nice and cuddly, customer-loving and smiley. The second is a bad-tempered, suspicious, customer-hating grump. Unfortunately, most banks display the second character more often than the first, but both exist and it is managing this schizophrenia in a way that ensures the second character is suppressed that is the secret of success for a few banks. However, no-one makes money out of being nice, so does it matter whether a bank is dominated by the grump or the smiley?

I'm not sure.

The conversation came to light as I discussed hiring policies with a small group of bankers last week. The head of one major UK bank known for its great customer service was saying how they had changed policy over the years from hiring based on experience to hiring based upon attitude. Does the person engage in a warm conversation, are they focused upon the individual they are talking with, do they show empathy, etc. The more ticks in boxes the person has for the right customer facing attitudes, the more likely they are to get the job.

Now I use this bank's services and can confirm that, on the telephone, they have one of the best telephone manners of any firm I deal with, not just in banking but across the board.

They're brilliant. But they're tiny by comparison with most banks that I use.

No-one makes money out of being nice.

The main banks I use are obvious grumps. They disempower their staff from any decision-making capability. Everything is carefully controlled and counted, from the use of paper clips to toilet paper in the branch loos. All processes and operations are costed, timed, ticked and notarised.

It's all about control. This bank wants operational efficiency and cost-income ratio to be the best in the industry. The first bank's cost-income ratio is over 60% and is unsustainable. The second bank's cost-income ratio is under 40% and it makes money for its shareholders.

No-one makes money out of being nice.

It's Banking Jim, But Not As We Know It

Strangely enough, the controlling bank is the one that wins out every time which is why most banks want staff to remove their brains before entering the office. You can't have staff with attitude or who use their brains to engage customers in a frank and open dialogue. After all, they may make a boo-boo by telling the customer they're right. They shouldn't have had those charges. Yes, your overdraft fee is steep, we'll waive it this time.

That's not operational efficiency. The control is not there. You can't have empowerment with control. The two are mutually exclusive. Or so the view goes.

No-one makes money out of being nice.

This is why banks are all about process management, workflow controls, strict rules and procedures. Banking is about risk and security, not engagement and openness. Allowing free rein to emotional engagement with customers through staff that create experiences is therefore anathema for most banks, as no-one makes money out of being nice.

Equally, it is why banks are not focused upon innovation, as innovation implies entrepreneurialism, imagination, creativity and risk ... these are all things that a bank needs to suppress as that does not deliver security, control and efficiency. In fact, innovation does the opposite.

All in all therefore, a bank is not a schizophrenic. A bank is about control, security and efficiency.

It is not about being smiley, warm and engaging. So stuff Mr. Smiley and hello Mr. Grump.

That's the bank I deal with and, like it or lump it, it's the bank we deserve.

Just being average is good enough (2008)

We had a huge bust-up last night, when a banking colleague and I were discussing customer service. Over dinner, we were all recounting stories of good and bad customer services, and boy did we have a few humdingers.

The change of address where the telecoms firm didn't do the switchover on the day you requested, so you ring up and they say that they got the dates mixed up but it will be fine ... in a week or two. The utilities firm that you called to explain that the person living at the household was a relative who is now deceased. "Oh no", comes the reply, "we can only deal with the account holder!" The retailer who delivers on the wrong day, so you call them up and they say that you ordered it through their internet service, and dispatch received the wrong date because the date was called through from the store. And the bank which you call and ask to change a payments mandate, and they change the wrong mandate. Sure, we had plenty of horror stories to tell ... but then we are British, so we enjoy nothing better than a good whine and a moan.

The common thread was that, in these days of self-service, everything goes brilliantly ... as long as you can do it yourself.

The positive stories were all about how wonderful it is to use services such as Amazon, eBay, PayPal, online ticketing services and Internet banking, because you are in control. You can make sure it is always right. However, the issues always occur when something goes wrong with the process. Maybe you entered the wrong information, or maybe you didn't self-serve but used a human – yes, a human! – to help you. Typically, things were then messed up because humans screw-up the process. All of our horror stories were about trying to change something through a human interface.

It's Banking Jim, But Not As We Know It

Then the banker in our group piped up, and said, "That's because we only want to be good enough to be average." "Pardon," we all exclaimed. "Well look, it's simple," he responded. "Banks, utility firms, telcos and more, we all just want to deal with the average."

We all looked puzzled, so he continued. "To ensure our costs are as low as they can be and our income as high as it can be, we all cater for the average customer. We know that, for the average customer, we get things right around 90% of the time. We know that, for the average customer, when we get things wrong, 90% of them will not do anything about it. And we know that, for the ones who will do something about it, 90% of them will complain and only a few will actually take action. Those few are now 0.1% of the customer base, and it's not worth spending thousands to cater for the few, as it would undermine the cost base.

"So go ahead, get angry. We don't care, because it's good enough for us to be average for the average customer."

We all looked a bit shocked. In fact, we all looked a bit like something had just died as we went through the emotions of grief: anger, fear, depression and finally acceptance.

"Ye Gods," we chimed, "if you're right then good service is bad for business!"

"No," he said. "You need to deliver as good a service as the average competitor, as you would have more than 0.1% reach the action stage if you were always below market average. But you balance good service over costs, good service over the competition, good service over customer retention and good service over bad business. It's all about balance and being average."

So there you have it.

Strangely enough, I remember reading Fred Reichheld's book, 'The Loyalty Effect', a decade ago and it focused upon customer advocacy and how poorly serviced customers will tell 10 of their friends, whilst well serviced customers will only tell a couple.

What Reichheld missed out in that book is that the ones who complain to their mates will only find that their mates all say "They're all like that", as we did last night. Not one of us could point to a bank, telco, utility firm or retailer with a defence that said: "Look, these guys are an exception to the rule." And the ones who tried to do that by naming a few firms, just got shot down in flames by the rest of us, who had some horror story to share about them, too.

So maybe we should just shoot for the average?

Or maybe we should do what Fred Reichheld now says, according to the comment by Ian Buckley on my Wells Fargo blog. Ian says: "Just reading a book called 'The Ultimate Question', which is about Net Promoter Score. In his introduction, the author, (Fred Reichheld) talks about good profits and bad profits. The later are gleaned from marketing, sales or pricing 'tricks' and tend to be short-lived. Good profits are sustainable. They come from the 'Golden Rule' of treating customers, as you yourself would like to be treated. This Golden Rule is the key to long-term, sustainable business growth."

How true.

Which brings me back to where I started. Good service stories today, are all about self-service because then you can treat the customer as you would like to be treated yourself.

Game, set and match.

You don't have to be big to rule my world ... (2008)

I realised that there's a link between average being good enough, and large global banks.

The link is that HSBC, Citi, Deutsche and more, are all aiming to provide a single, global platform – One Bank – with consistent, global delivery to all bank, corporate and high net worth clients.

Sure, there are retail operations, but these can be far more delineated to the culture and structure of the local needs. The large cross-border clients however, want consistent global service and, for these, average is good enough.

But here, I don't mean 'average'. It can still be great service, as evidenced by many of the comments such as Kevin Lodge's: "The underlying assumption is that good service costs money. However, if you take the opposite track that good service should save you money (and reduce your customers' costs) then a whole new world of possibilities opens up."

That is what the major global players are doing. They are focusing upon LCD: the Lowest Common Denominator (not Liquid Crystal Display).

LCD for a global operation can be measured in calls responded to in less than 30 seconds, customer issues resolved on first contact, new account openings online and through branch and so on. The same measures you might have in a country operation.

But for a global operation that wants to deliver consistent global service, this means that every branch, every customer service rep, every manager, works to and is able to deliver against a common set of rules and service level agreements (SLAs). These SLAs target to attain the LCD for the bank (not against the competition) and are then pushed through globally.

The result is that the bank can honestly say that for clients with cross-border needs, they are guaranteed a minimum LCD. This minimum LCD can be targeted to be as good as or better than the competitors, but it must be the average for the Group. Any deviation from the norm should be managed.

That's what McDonalds, Marriott and others do. A minimum, guaranteed level of service. Then anything above the norm is cream on the cake! And the whole lot of course can be managed by global technology dashboards that the CEOs can use to leverage down or up on service, costs, revenues and margins. The result is consistent, global service to a minimum service level (SLA to the LCD), and you're onto a winner. No wonder these guys are building single, global technology platforms to deliver (and measure) all this stuff!

Equally, what this should mean for domestic and regional players, is focus upon the extra value-adds you can target above the LCD. That's the relationship management bits, for sure, but it's more than that. After all, the global players have relationship managers.

It's more to do with very localised and targeted services.

After all, if the large global guys want to go for LCD with SLAs on a globalised basis, why not go for HDD: Highest Differentiated Delivery (not Hard Disk Drives!).

That means localised knowledge, localised systems, localised service, localised delivery ... yes, the global guys can do this but, if they are delivering on a global, single platform for efficiency and effectiveness, give them a shot of the old David and Goliath and concentrate on what you can do to differentiate locally using localised platforms.

There will always be competition, and always big guys versus small guys. The game always comes down to who is the nimbler, faster, stronger, more capable ... and that can sometimes be the small guy.

Come on, you little guys!

We don't need your customer service (2009)

For a while now Monitise, the mobile payments processing firm, has been researching views on the future of banking with the Future Foundation, part of Experian.

Their objective is to find out how our relationship with money is changing and to understand how the culture of money will develop over the next few years.

The first research report was published last December, and focused upon the mobile internet and what that would mean for financial providers.

The second report came out in May 2009, and concluded that "consumers, led by young people, are migrating away from cash and towards digital transactions. The overwhelming benefit of convenience underpins the appeal of digital transactions and so does a deepening sense of trust in the technology."

The latest report finds that Britons prefer doing their own banking, and would deliberately choose a computer or a mobile phone to manage their finances before phoning a call centre. They don't want to deal with people in other words – whether in branches or call centres - but want to self-service wherever and whenever possible.

Key results include:

◆ One in five of us would prefer to log-on than dial a call centre and speak to a person;

◆ This preference has grown rapidly – up from 1 in 20 in 2002 – as technology has improved and broadband become more widespread;

◆ Unsurprisingly, it is the younger generation leading the way – with more than a quarter of 18 to 25 year-olds opting for technology ahead of the human touch;

◆ Pensioners are also getting in on the do-it-yourself act, with one in 10 logging-on or using their mobile phone to manage their money instead of the call centre;

◆ Fulfilling gender stereotypes, more men than women said that a major benefit of using technology to do their own banking was the lack of other people (22% compared to 13%).

The latest report was produced by the Future Foundation asking 1,000 adults in the UK for their views on the role of technology in customer service. All in all, it made me think it's just another hole in The Wall ...

Customer:

"We don't want no human service,

We don't want your bank controls.

No charges or fees on my accounts,

Banker, leave my cash alone.

Hey Banker! Leave my cash alone.

All in all, I only want ...

Another hole in the wall."

And, after a comment on silo-based functions in banks the other day, I thought that bankers could respond with:

"We don't want no integration,

We don't want no consistency.

No surly clients in the branch rooms,

Customer, leave those tweets alone.

Hey Customer! Leave those tweets alone.

All in all, please just use ...

Another hole in the wall."

Corporates, as with individuals, just want relationships (2008)

A recent discussion at the Financial Services Club had the interesting title 'What do corporates really want from their bank?', with four business managers talking about their banking needs.

Although the four gentlemen are heads of business and finance at firms of varying sizes and complexity, with varying needs for financial support, they all had a common thread: corporates want their banks to understand them; they want a relationship; they want good service. No more and no less.

Whether you are a pensioner with £75 in your account; or a small business with £75 million turnover per annum; or a major corporation turning over £75 billion a year; you want to be understood. You want to deal with banks that focus upon your business, understand it, pre-empt your requirements with appropriate offers and proactively advise you on how to get the best out of your banking services.

Strangely enough, none of the corporates at the table felt that banks did this very well, however … except one.

The small businesses, for example, felt that bank advisory services and focus upon SMEs were sorely lacking something. The first speaker was the managing director of a call centre management firm. He began by explaining how his firm had grown from nothing to a multi-million pound business. He felt that the banks were very poor at educating people like him on financial matters that are appropriate to SMEs. For example, he wants to go on the acquisition trail but has no idea how to do this and does not know who to talk with.

This is something that I have seen being addressed by websites such as Fortis's Join2Grow but overall, yes, this is still weak across the banking sector generally.

Next was the managing director of a security and logistics organisation, who expanded upon this theme by saying that there was a distinct moment for him when the banking relationship changed from one of no interest to one of hard sell. That moment was the first year his firm broke through the £50 million ($100 million) turnover level. He felt that when his firm broke the £50 million a year turnover level, the banks moved from showing no interest in lending money to him, to one where they were falling over themselves trying to give the firm money.

132

His comment overall was that the banks were letting themselves down, as he wants them to understand the business and its staff, and to show how the bank can make a difference, as they grow from an SME into a corporate; not just to turn up when they have grown up and become a corporate and then try to squeeze interest and fees out of them.

The group treasurer of a major airline spoke next. He believed that FX management, currency risks and core cash management are the main requirements for a business of his size. Equally, they have a large volume of aircraft to manage, as well as complex leasing arrangements. These are the main managed services they are provided for through the bank, although they had found it incredibly difficult to get structured finance. All of these challenges he felt the banks were doing a good enough job with, but could do better.

Finally, the head of information security for a major satellite TV network felt that his challenge was fraud, with identity theft being the key issue. The fact that more money is being made through cybercrime than from drug dealing is a major challenge for the industry, and specifically for his business, and he wanted to know that the bank holding the firm's money is secure and not at risk of loss.

So, the overall themes of what corporates really want from the banks is advice on finance, security of their money, nurturing and supporting their business, and being proactive in identifying opportunities to be more efficient and profitable. All traits that they felt the industry is providing, but not as well as it could.

I thought the airline treasurer probably gave one of the best summaries of the overall situation, as he stated that the relationship is essential. "I need to know who to call and when and consumer call centre issues are the same as corporate call centre issues: we need to be able to talk to someone we know."

This is so simple – the fact that banking is about service and service is based upon relationships between humans – and yet, it is so often forgotten.

He elaborated on this point by stating that he is continually being called by "banks that want to do business, especially as (the airline) requires a lot of FX dollar processing. The trouble is that once the banks are in there working with us, they always want to sell more".

Now there's a surprise.

He concluded by saying that "The banks that work are those who talk about our business and advise us. For example, we are now working with one bank that had no business with (the airline) a few years ago, but we now process over a third of our transactions with this bank because they do that."

Oh, I bet we all wish we were that bank … and yet, we all could be that bank if we just remember that banking is about service, and service is based upon people having good relationships with people.

Relationships are based upon listening and caring, a bit like a marriage. Those that listen, care and respond the most attentively and appropriately on a consistent basis, will always win more business and have a longer-term relationship, than those who just want to have a one-night stand.

Chapter 7 Marketing in the new media age

Introduction

Finally, let's talk about marketing to the new generation customer. Marketing in my day was all about billboards, TV and newspaper ads, airtime and one-way broadcasting. Marketing today is all about dialogue, discussion, debate and diatribes via new media such as Twitter, Facebook, YouTube and apps. For some banks, this offers great reach and great opportunity as they can see how to use these services to market their bank for free. Other banks have no idea what this new media means, and have yet to remove the firewalls that blinker their thinking. Marketing today should be all about honest and open communications with your community of participants – or that's what it will be tomorrow – so remove those blinkers fast or you just might become a former bank.

And the best brand in the world is ... Chinese (2010)

Fascinating report in the FT this week about global brands, with the financial sector bouncing back the strongest of all. MasterCard and Visa led the financial pack, although Goldman Sachs saw a 25% growth in brand value over the last year ... I wonder how much they lost this year?

Anyways, considering banks had the worst results ever last year and lost all brand momentum, it's no surprise I guess to see they've bounced back this year, and even beat beer as a sector for brand improvements.

(...)

All in all, a big contrast between this and the Harris Interactive Reputation Survey. So brands and reputation have nothing to do with each other, do they?

What surprised me is the list of the top 10 brands in our sector.

Financial Institutions – Top 20 by brand value						
Rank	Brand	Brand value $m	Brand contribution	Brand momentum	Brand value change	Two-year CAGR
1	ICBC	43.927	4	7	15%	11%
2	Visa	24.883	5	9	52%	NA
3	HSBC	23.408	4	3	23%	6%
4	Bank of China	21.960	3	6	4%	3%
5	China Construction Bank	20.929	3	7	-8%	3%
6	Wells Fargo	18.746	5	7	16%	-5%
7	Santander	18.012	3	9	12%	7%
8	RBC	16.608	5	9	12%	-2%
9	Bank of America	16.393	2	9	6%	-15%
10	ICICI	14.454	1	9	NA	NA
11	American Express	13.912	3	3	-7%	-13%
12	Citi	13.403	2	7	-8%	17%
13	BBVA	12.977	5	9	3%	10%
14	Chase	12.426	4	9	17%	0%
15	MasterCard	11.659	5	7	57%	15%
16	TD	10.274	5	7	-7%	NA
17	Goldman Sachs	9.283	4	9	25%	-6%
18	Barclays	8.383	1	7	20%	4%
19	US Bank	8.377	5	8	NA	NA
20	Standard Chartered	8.327	2	6	1%	5%

Source *Millward Brown Optimor (including from BrandZ, Datamonitor and Bloombergitor and Bloomberg)*

It's Banking Jim, But Not As We Know It

Wow! ICBC from China, the #1 bank brand in the world! In fact, they're the 11th best brand in the world, just behind Google and Apple.

Proof that (UK) banks miss out on new media marketing (2009)

If you want proof that UK banks miss out on new media, you only need to look at *Revolution*'s annual awards for 2009.

Revolution magazine is one of my favourite monthly reads, as it's all about innovation online. Each year their awards ceremony recognises the best of British internet marketing across a range of categories, from best use of search engines to email, from mobile to websites, from using virals to much more.

This year's Awards magazine landed on my doorstep today and I counted 48 nominations in eight cross-industry categories. Eight winners, nine highly commended companies and 31 short-listed organisations. All industries represented, and all selected for being good online.

Guess what? Not one bank. None of the cross-industry categories has a single bank recognised or even shortlisted.

There are four financial firms in the 48, although not one winner. And the four financial entrants were:

◆   More Th>n Business, shortlisted for best B2B campaign;
◆   Tesco Personal Finance, shortlisted for best use of search;
◆   Experian, shortlisted for best use of email; and
◆   Swiftcover mobile, shortlisted for best use of mobile.

There was also a specific category for best Financial Services use of the web. That one was won by an insurance company, the Prudential, for their targeting of retirement planning through an interactive service.

A bank doesn't even win in its own industry!

Barclays was highly commended for its student campaign, and NatWest was shortlisted for its personal banking website.

Illustration: Barclays launched a movie competition on YouTube for students in October 2007. The competition was to make a video of a famous movie scene to win free access to the cinema for a year. With the competition finished, I went and had a look at Barclays Student Group on YouTube, and it has seven videos, five of which were made by Barclays and two are older videos that students entered.

I applaud Barclays for trying, but if that's the best in our industry ...

Compare these with the two 'leaders' of Nike who won the innovation award, and Orange who won the Grand Prix prize, and it's like comparing the Model T Ford with the latest Formula 1 racing vehicles.

I know I'm having a rant, but it's a poor show when banking, a business based upon bits and bytes, doesn't have a clue how to use bits and bytes to grow business and reach customers.

Thank gawd banks overseas have some clue.

For example, the Financial Brand posted a great insight yesterday entitled: 'Differentiation: the key to branding'. The message?

"You must be different. If you can't actually be different, at least look different. Differentiation – even if only achieved on a cosmetic and superficial level – will at least get you noticed, and that's the first step on the way to building a strong brand."

Ten comments had been posted so far, and one is from Fernando Egido Egaña who says:

"At CAN (Caja Navarra, Spain, a truly innovative bank) we think that differentiation leads to more different results: economic ones and more far-reaching ones. We have developed a new business model called Civic Banking. Based on the promotion of (new and extended) rights, we want to be leaders in civic finances, so that CAN becomes a benchmark for social and financial innovation. Take a look to our website http://www.cajanavarra.es/en where you will find more information about us."

So I took a look at their website, and Fernando is right. The CAN site is a good, informative website. It's multilingual, interactive and instructive. And it has a strong message about why CAN is worth dealing with through a strong focus upon connection with community.

Like other Spanish banks, such as BBVA, I see innovations in new media in parts of Europe.

Why not in the UK, which is one of the most wired countries in the EU?

Congratulations to Dexia for some new bank thinking (2010)

Thanks to the Italian blog Banca2.0, I stumbled across Dexia Belgium's marketing campaign to Gen Y that worked wonders almost a year ago.

The campaign is based around Dexia's youth bank, Axion, and the bank's aim was to appeal to 15- to 30-year old Belgians by highlighting music as the theme.

But not just any old music: web music.

The bank used media agency Boondoggle to come up with a brilliant campaign whereby an internet 'banner ad' styled stage was built, and then a bunch of well-known Belgian bands were filmed to kick-start the competition.

The competition? Oh yeah, the competition is based on the premise that there are so many struggling bands out there on MySpace and YouTube, why not give them a showcase?

They've produced a campaign backing this. The text ran:

"Banks and youngsters.

It's not really love at first sight.

They try to win your heart and wallet by giving you ...

... a free sports bag!

But what if a bank actually did something meaningful for young people?

Wouldn't that be a better way of connecting with future customers?

Axion is a Belgian bank (and division of Dexia) that decided to really support youngsters.

In one of the most important aspects of their life: music.

The past few years, there's been an ever increasing number of young bands, trying in vain for MySpace fame.

In a time when the international music industry is struggling to survive, Axion decided it was time to give these young bands a little push.

We created an internet first: "Banner Concerts".

We built boxes in exactly the same scale as online banners.

We invited well-known Belgian bands to perform live in the boxes, and filmed their concerts.

We played these videos as the first Banner Concerts ever.

Each banner led to the Banner Concerts website: the first website that consisted of nothing but banners. On the website, you could enter your own band's work, to try to win your very own Banner Concert.

We raised extra awareness by spreading posters in music and CD stores, bars and restaurants ...

... broadcasting commercials on MTV and TMF, and sending out emails."

In the second phase of the campaign, a jury selected 25 bands out of 255 entries, and went back to the studios to record 25 new Banner Concerts videos. The 25 new Banner Concerts were

It's Banking Jim, But Not As We Know It

heavily promoted, with the winning bands on lots of other websites, and the public got to vote for which was the very best Banner Concert.

The bands themselves were also very creative about promoting their work on social networking sties. And the winning band – Bad Cirkuz – won a recording session and a real gig at Ancienne Belgique, one of Belgium's biggest concert halls.

The results:

◆　25 young bands got an exposure for their live gig via 6,807,442 banner impressions on Belgium's most popular websites and, by providing an embed option, a further 43,479 impressions were generated on fan pages and blogs.

◆　Between October and December 2008, 44,845 unique visitors went to the Banner Concerts website and, between December 1st and 10th, 7,581 people voted for their favourite Banner Concert.

And that's how the advertising space of a bank became the advertising space of a band.

Halifax's marketing is the worst I've ever seen ... (2010)

Every time the new Halifax ad comes on the box, I cringe ...

Now I've blogged about their awful advertising before and how insensitive it seems post-crisis, but this one really gets me down. Not only is it cheesy, poorly executed and raw, but it actually makes most of the folks I talk to feel sick to see a bank that has cost billions in bailouts advertising as though nothing has changed.

And I'm not alone as the *Telegraph* decided to run a page asking what readers thought about a bank that offered a reward of £5 as long as you deposit a minium £1,000 per month. This advertising seems a bit rich, the *Telegraph* claims, when this particular bank has cost each and every family in Britain £5,500 to bail out in the last two years.

Steve Griffiths, director of brand and customer marketing for Halifax, says that their new advertising campaign focuses on "the core message that Halifax rewards its customers for their business and shows that our colleagues are enthusiastic, friendly and approachable".

The *Telegraph's* readers say:

> "Never mind the advert, I want my £5,500 back. I need it more than they do."

> "Who ever authorised this at Halifax needs stringing up for crimes against society!"

> "Look closely and it really does show them up as a bank that can't be trusted."

> "Rather than coming across as 'friendly and approachable' they come across as a load of immature bumbling morons."

> "If they changed the tune to 'sorry seems to be the hardest word' then maybe, just maybe, there might be some mileage in this. Talk about misreading the mood of the country."

(...)

Most worryingly for Steve Griffiths, director of brand and customer marketing for Halifax, should be the comments that read:

> "I bank with the Halifax and this advert makes me want to leave them. It is that annoying!"

> "Absolutely atrocious! Makes me want to change my bank!"

> "I am embarrassingly a Halifax customer, but not for long, I couldn't handle people knowing I bank with such morons, & that's not counting the £39 they charge you for an email for a £2.50 failed payment."

It's Banking Jim, But Not As We Know It

"What the advert doesn't mention is the £12.50 per month which they charge you just for having the account, which of course does not include the overdraft charges of £1 per day, the £1.50 per month 'debit card fee', and anything else they can think of to sting you with."

Message to Halifax: start advertising with honesty and sensitivity, and stop advertising as though the great British public are numbskulls believing that nothing has happened.

What the Halifax should have done ... (2010)

Thinking about the Halifax's ads a bit more, some may say: "they are so bad, they're good". I disagree. The Halifax ads are just plain bad and have been well past their sell-by date for a long time.

For example, Delaney Lund Knox Warren & Partners (DLKW) won the Halifax account ten years ago and has run the 'cast of characters' campaign – the one with staff members such as Howard – ever since.

Ten years is a long time for any campaign, particularly a cheesy one that has seen the bank bankrupted two years ago and now trading under new ownership, 43% of which is taxpayer-funded.

So what should the bank have done? How about a bit of honesty? Run a campaign called: "we're sorry".

Get a serious but consumer-liked presenter, pay him/her a big chunk of money and get him/her to be a talking head.

Then I would script him to say something like:

"The credit crisis has affected everyone, and the Halifax has been a part of that. They are sorry about this and, to recognise their gratitude to their customers they are rewarding every customer with a £5 payment for making a deposit of £1,000 each month. This is to reflect the fact that they have changed.

They thank you for your continued support and guess what? I think they are OK, so give them a try."

Something far more genuflective, like this, would be received so much better than using a 10 year-old, tired campaign.

Tesco, Virgin, O2 and all ... we don't want your banks (2009)

Marketing Week ran a fascinating survey of British citizens last month and their views about banking. The results find that most people don't trust trusted brands with their money, and would rather stick with the banks.

The survey sampled 1,716 UK adults and asked a series of questions, including...

Which, if any, of the following brands would you consider taking out a financial product with (e.g. credit card, savings account, current account)?

None of these	65%
Tesco Finance	20%
M&S Money	18%
Sainsbury's Bank	15%
A charity you support	6%
ICICI	4%
O2	3%
B&Q	1%
Pizza Express	1%

These results surprised me, with 65% of consumers saying they would not take out a financial product with any of their favourite brands. I was also shocked as Tesco, M&S and Sainsbury have been in banking and financial services for over a decade. After 10 years, can it be true that people really don't trust these trusted brands? What would the score be for Virgin, another major brand that has been digging into this space for a decade?

It's Banking Jim, But Not As We Know It

This was no more surprising than the shock result of the next question ...

What are the most important features that you look for in your main financial provider?

Easy/convenient banking online	41%
Competitive interest rates	39%
Security	37%
Overall stability of the financial institution	34%
Reasonable and non–punitive fees	24%
Error-free management of accounts	22%
Convenient branch network	17%
Well established financial services brand	16%
Treating me like an individual	15%
Friendly and easily accessible staff	15%
Don't know	5%

The number one answer is easy and convenient online banking? Wow! Only a few years ago, most people would have said that they weren't interested in banking online due to issues over reason number three – security. Amazing what broadband access can do isn't it? Mind you, with online banking used by four out of five households these days, maybe it's not so surprising.

Then they asked which statements folks agree with, and these were quite surprising (or not) too ....

- Both individuals and companies have taken on too much risk for short-term gain (62%);

- It's easy to feel you're no longer in financial control (59%);

- It's hard to know who to trust in the world of financial uncertainty (53%);

- Banks don't care about the person behind the money (52%);

- Too interested in new customers, banks have forgotten the basics (50%);
- Banks are too focused upon profits and shareholders to have customers' interests at heart (49%);
- Too complicated and confusing means I switch off (20%);
- I get more out of spending money than saving it (17%).

I can understand the first three statements, but these results mean that every other customer of a bank thinks that their bank is not interested in them as a person or as a customer. Wow! So why do they stay? Why don't they switch? Maybe it's because 1 in 20 have no idea why they chose their bank ... or maybe it's because, as the editor of *Marketing Week* writes, "A month ago I changed my bank. I'm already fighting with the new people in charge of my money over £70-worth of what I consider to be unwarranted charges."

There's quite a few other worthwhile things to quote from the article too, such as Philip Mehl, Head of Marketing for HSBC UK, who says: "We have avoided jumping on to the bandwagon of telling customers how to run their lives better in a recession, as we have learned that customers want banks to run their own businesses better before we start throwing out unsolicited advice."

Jeez ... a banker talking sense. Stick that in your diary.

The article about the survey has a number of classic lines too.

> "It seems that while marketers are always told that trust in brands equates to commercial success, the financial sector does not appear to follow this rule. In a Morgan Stanley survey published last week, consumers claim they trust Tesco more than the banks and believe it offers better value. But a third stated they 'definitely wouldn't' or were 'very unlikely' to open a Tesco current account and this figure rose to half when it came to taking out a Tesco mortgage."

Mmmm ... that's good news for the launch of Tesco Bank, isn't it?

It's Banking Jim, But Not As We Know It

"When looking at which words consumers associate with their main bank, 'loyalty' and 'acceptance' rate highly while words like 'anger' and 'contempt' receive just a fraction of responses in comparison."

So, the media are wrong about the general populace hating their banks then?

The article then gets into some case studies with banks and non-banks, with some fascinating conversation with Alistair Johnston, O2's marketing director:

"We're acutely aware the communications sector around voice and text has reached its [full] size and, if we're going to grow the business, then we have to find new areas ... we think we can offer new ways to manage money. In the future, people will be walking around with their phones, they won't have cards or wallets", he says. That's why O2 have launched a couple of payments cards, as have Phones4U, to test the waters of banking.

Even so, this is not necessarily the biggest concern for big banks. Their concern should be customers switching to small banks.

"Co-operative Financial Services claims it has seen a 'massive increase' in customers switching from the big names to smaller ones. Specifically, in comparison to last year, there has been a 636% increase in RBS customers switching, 236% in HBOS and 165% in Lloyds TSB."

Yowzer! What does this mean for the big banks?

Maybe take a tip out of HSBC's flagship customer brand, First Direct?

"First Direct head of digital marketing Joan Sutherland explains: '86% of all our transactions are now online, so our biggest challenge is how to replicate the fantastic rapport our reps developed with customers on the phone and inject the brand personality into the online space.'"

What did they do?

Lots of personalisation including the social media newsroom and Virtual Forest, a place where customers get to plant a tree for every time 20 accounts switch to paperless banking. They also focused heavily on the mobile space, with 500,000 hits on the website from iPhones so far this year to July.

All in all, it's about innovation, which brings me back to Philip Mehl of HSBC.

> "The tendency in any recession is to go into lockdown mode and this is precisely not what we have done. First, if you don't invest for growth, when it does arrive you'll be slow to take advantage of it and second, innovation can take time to come on-stream so it needs to be planned well ahead."

I told you he talked sense, didn't I?

We know where you are (2009)

Only two years ago, many technology companies and banks were talking about the branch of the future and painting a vision where, when you walked into a branch, the branch sensors would pick up who you were using RFID and NFC technologies from your contactless debit or credit card.

The result would be a warm "Welcome Mr. Skinner" as you opened the branch door, combined with an interactive advert on the branch television screens screaming: "Chris, don't you need a new mortgage?"

As I walk up to the teller, he or she would then say, "Hello Mr. Skinner, we thought you might be interested in this new mortgage offer at just 0.5% interest for 50 years. Here's your personalised brochure with all the details".

Today, that vision has gone away. Few folks talk about using contactless chips for proximity marketing – they're all now focused upon mobile telephony – and the personalised brochures scream "Lend us money or lose your house".

149

Whatever.

But we should be clear that the idea of the personalisation of marketing, and particularly financial marketing, will not disappear.

Just yesterday, Google were all over the news again for their increasingly intrusive approach to online advertising. This time, they are using your surfing habits to provide targeted advertising based upon your internet viewing. In my case, I'd get non-stop ads for "Lend us money or lose your house", because they know I visit financial websites.

In fact, Google are all around us with their ubiquitous observations, from Google Street View to Google Earth to Google Mail to Google Search.

From a privacy viewpoint, another controversial Google technology was the recent introduction of Google Latitude, which monitors your friends, family and other associates as they walk around town, using GSM tracking of the mobile phone in their pocket.

Monitoring people's movements using GSM and soon to be pervasive 3G technologies will become a standard, and the idea of banks and financial firms ignoring such opportunities for marketing services is blatant idiocy.

Thus far though, there has not been much evidence of proximity-based marketing of finance using mobile technologies.

There was the example of a bank that used Bluetooth technologies to sense potential customers walking past branches and sent a text message saying "Walk in now for cheap loans", but that experiment failed when the technology sent the message to everyone walking past the branch.

And yet, think of the potential for such servicing.

You leave the firm with a big fat redundancy cheque, and the first thing you see is a digital ad on the side of a lorry saying: "Mr. Skinner, that cheque could be worth twice as much this time next year if you join our Ponzi scheme".

As you walk past the car showroom, a targeted ad says: "buy a new 4-door today with 0% financing from the bank that loves ya".

Or you leave the casino with empty pockets, and a sign pops up at the bus stop shouting: "Chris, ya big loser. Get back in there by texting 'yes' to 80088 BANK for another $10,000 stake".

The possibilities are endless and yes, have been considered for a long time. But we always then wonder about the privacy issues.

"Oh, err, will the customer feel happy about us sending an advert for more money as they leave the brothel?" are the heart-rending debates in the corridors of marketers of money everywhere.

"Sure", says the Head of Proximity-based Experiential Marketing (HOP'EM for short), "anything that gives them an extra buck!"

You see, privacy is irrelevant in today's socially networked world. In this world, nothing is private anyway. We're CCTV captured every other step of our meanderings around cities and, if I want to, I can find out anyone's email address, telephone number, spouse, children, siblings, parents, uncles, aunts, cousins, friends and business associates just by drilling down through the poorly managed privacy layers of Facebook, MySpace and Twitter. Not forgetting Google, of course. Nothing is private. So privacy is no barrier from the customer's perspective.

From the bank's perspective it will be a barrier though, as the bank does not want to be seen to be playing footloose and fancy-free with customer data. So all you do is put a few tick boxes on the clients' mobile bank account application form saying: "Would you like us to improve our mobile financing services by sending you adverts that are relevant, rather than the junk rubbish you received a minute ago asking if you would like child educational bonds when we know you don't have children?" That way they're sure to sign up.

It's Banking Jim, But Not As We Know It

Banks are considering and some are deploying mobile proximity marketing services and, within a decade, most organisations will be in there running such services.

Just make sure you are one of them and that, as you deploy such marketing, you do it in a considerate manner. After all, we wouldn't want your eagle-eyed marketing to be an enemy of the state now, would we?

Should banks stop advertising? (2009)

February's *The Banker* magazine dropped onto my doorstep this morning with the front page: 'The World's Top 500 Banking Brands'.

You might be surprised that there are 500 banks around these days but this is worldwide, and the top ones are pretty obvious (last year's position in brackets):

1	(1)	HSBC (UK)
2	(3)	Bank of America (USA)
3	(8)	Wells Fargo (USA)
4	(4)	Santander (Spain)
5	(16)	ICBC (China)
6	(5)	American Express (USA)
7	(2)	Citi (USA)
8	(7)	BNP Paribas (France)
9	(18)	China Construction Bank (China)
10	(6)	Chase (USA)

There are a few other interesting movements in there such as:
- Bradesco, Brazil – up from 42nd to 12th
- Banco Itau, Brazil – up from 54th to 21st
- Shinsei Bank, Japan – up from 230th to 142nd

While big losers include:

- Bank of Ireland, Ireland – down 98 places from 61st to 159th
- OTP Bank, Hungary – down 109 places from 67th to 176th
- AIFUL, Japan – down from number 168 to 418th
- e*trade, USA – down from 246 to position 458

I won't go through the process the magazine used, you'll have to buy it to find that out, but it does seem to imply that most American and European bank brands are falling in value whilst the BRIC (Brazilian, Russian, Indian and Chinese) bank brands are on the rise.

This concurs with a few other branding rankings I spotted, such as Millward Brown's 2008 BrandZ report 2008:

> "The overall brand value of financial institutions increased despite challenges faced by British and US banks because of the sub-prime crisis. In contrast, Chinese banks have experienced two consecutive years of growth. It is hard to tell how much of this success is driven by good management and how much by favourable economic conditions. Chinese banks brands also benefited from recent IPOs that strengthened the bond between brands and their shareholders."

In their top 100 brands (*The Banker* positions in brackets):

Bank rank	Overall rank	
1	14	Bank of America, brand value up 15% (2)
2	15	Citi, down 10% (7)
3	18	ICBC, up 70% (5)
4	20	American Express, up 7% (6)
5	21	Wells Fargo, up 2% (3)
6	31	China Construction Bank, up 31% (9)
7	32	Bank of China, up 42% (15)
8	34	Royal Bank of Canada, up 39% (27)
9	35	HSBC, up 6% (1)
10	42	Deutsche Bank, up 14% (17)

It's Banking Jim, But Not As We Know It

Meanwhile, in the most well-known branding list, Interbrand places the banks as follows:

Bank rank	Overall rank	
1	15	American Express, up 5%
2	19	Citi, down 14%
3	27	HSBC, down 3%
4	34	Merrill Lynch, down 21%
5	37	JP Morgan, down 6%
6	38	Goldman Sachs, down 3%
7	41	UBS, down 11%
8	42	Morgan Stanley, down 16%
9	86	ING, down 3%
10	100	Visa, new entry

I left out Thomson Reuters, Allianz, AXA and a few others in the financial space as they are not included in *The Banker's* lists.

What this demonstrates is how rapidly bank brands are trashed and how painstakingly and costly they are to build.

For example, think about the number of airports, sports stadiums, leagues and music events that are sponsored by financial and banking brands. Now think of how you feel when you see them today.

Citi Field is the new $850 million baseball stadium being built for the New York Mets. Citi is paying $20 million a year for the next 20 years to have its name there in lights. Unlike AIG, which sponsors Manchester United, with sponsorship about to be withdrawn.

Meanwhile, RBS sponsors Europe's Six Nations Rugby tournament and have just renewed their four-year contract. The last action is understandable, as the bank uses the Six Nations to entertain their corporate clients ... mind you, a £5 million ($7 million) per year corporate entertainment bill may seem a bit excessive, considering the current state of said bank.

I could post so many more, but when even American Express's marketing and promotion expenditure is down 35% due to tumbling profits, there is going to be a big drop in bank advertising and branding. It does not mean that bank advertising disappears altogether, just that it gets a lot less in your face.

Even then, I wonder how much influence this has and whether the multimillion dollar budgets are really worth it. What I would do right now, if I owned the bank's marketing budget and we were struggling, is to focus upon creating the best Facebook page, MySpace blog or YouTube rant, and advertise the bank that way.

Use these sites as a method of advising on how to get through a credit crunch for your corporate and consumer clients. Use these facilities to tell everyone how you're managing your budgets these days to get through this crisis as cheaply as possible. Just use them to get a message out there that does not seem to be out there: we know you are angry with us and here's what we're doing about it.

After all, if your brand can lose 10%, 20% or even all of its brand equity in just a few months, thanks to the trashing of your balance sheet, then tighten the belt, show people you are doing so and get an honest message out there.

Bank brands ... forget the adverts (2008)

We had a great conversation about bank brands at the Asian Banker's Retail Excellence Program (I'm an advisor to the program and sit on the judging panel for their Awards). It started with Nielsen sharing some data about a branding analysis project they ran over the last year, covering 179 bank brands across Asia. The results looked at the Brand Equity Index (BEI) for each bank, with BEI being comprised of various features such as awareness, consideration, confidence, preference, recommendation, trust, reputation and so on.

As a result of looking at these factors, each bank is given a score between 1 and 10 based upon consumer surveys, e.g. if the consumer is aware of the bank brand, it gets 1; if they would consider that brand, it gets a score of 2; if they are confident of the brand, then a 3. You get the idea, e.g. a score of 10 is a really good score where you not only have a loyal customer, but an advocate who would recommend you to their friends and family.

A few did quite well, with the following named as stand-outs:

◆ DBS, Singapore;
◆ HSBC, Hong Kong;
◆ Kookmin Bank, South Korea;
◆ Siam Commercial Bank, Thailand ;
◆ State Bank of India, Indi.

Overall however, only three banks out of 179 across Asia scored more than 4; half scored less than 1; and the average score was 1.37. So much for all those dollars spent on marketing, eh?

My own view is that, although some banks do a good job of marketing their brands, most are pretty darned poor at it as this demonstrated. But the reason they are poor at it is that some think the brand is all about adverts, or 'mugs and mouse mats'. It's a marketing thing. Come up with nice tagline, like "the bank that likes to do well" and off you go.

To illustrate the point, I remember a US bank which hired a whizz marketer from a consumer goods company to run their bank branding programme. He came up with all sorts of stuff about the bank being "the people's bank", and they invested millions in a major branding campaign with TV spots and all sorts of other new brochureware.

Complete waste of money. The reason being that "the people's bank" had staff in branches who weren't that good at dealing with the people who came into the branch. They weren't "the people's bank", and the brand did not live up to its promise.

Bank brands are not cookies or cakes. They're people businesses. You can run a brand with a tagline if it's a fast moving consumer good (FMCG) because there are no people involved.

- "Just do it"
- "I'd like to teach the world to sing"
- "Quench the thirst"
- "Three blades, fewer strokes, less irritation"
- "Because you're worth it"
- "They're gggggggrrrrrrrrrrrrrrrrrrreat!"

I'm betting that you'll recognise at least one of those taglines, and could put the product to the line. That's brand marketing for FMCG. There are no humans involved, except in placing the line in your head, getting you to remember it, ensuring you therefore associate the positive line memory with the product when you see it in the store, and then hopefully that you buy it.

Now look at service industries.

- "The world's favourite airline"
- "The service, the quality, the spirit ... the experience ... it all begins here"
- "I'm lovin' it"

Each of these brand taglines – British Airways, Marriott Hotels and McDonald's in case you didn't recognise them – is making a promise that is only fulfilled when you touch the airline, hotel or restaurant. If you dislike the airline, cannot stand the service, and are hating it, then these dollars of advertising are wasted. Therefore, the staff have to make the airline the favourite; the service, quality and spirit of the hotel an experience; and cooking the food in a way that makes sure you are lovin' it each time, every time.

That is service industries marketing, and it is very precarious because it totally depends upon the people in these businesses delivering the brand promise. Any break in that brand promise

It's Banking Jim, But Not As We Know It

with the employee deliverer is the opportunity to waste your marketing efforts.

This is even more true for banks. For example, one bank here has the tagline: "We listen to and understand the needs our customers". If you promise that you listen to and understand my needs, and then I enter a branch or call your call centre and they are dismissive or lack knowledge, then you have wasted the marketing dollars.

This is the critical point and is illustrated by my own experience when running marketing for a business-to-business service provider. Many people could not understand why I spent over half of the available marketing budget on internal marketing materials, communications, education and training. But we were a services business. Our people are our advertisements. We do not need to put up billboards saying that we are good to work with. We just need to prove it, based upon excellent people, selling and delivering services to our customer's people through great relationships and trust.

This is as true for a consulting and systems integration business as it is for a bank, airline, hotel or restaurant. People delivering to people. Not people picking up a product off a shelf.

In the case of the technology service provider, if I advertise the promise 'excellence in delivery' and then we don't deliver excellence, then the marketing money is wasted. Promising 'excellence in delivery' is not just a line. It's a promise. We have to prove we live the line by having excellent people in delivery who understand what excellence means.

In services businesses, the people who engage the customers have to understand the marketing message means and bring it to life. They must not only hear the tune, but enjoy singing it. This is why service businesses cannot run brands that are taglines. They have to live the brand. The brand has to be the culture, not just an advert, or a mug or a mousemat.

This is why one of the best bank brand programmes I encountered was one that externally read, "We want to be your FIRST choice."

Not very impressive.

Behind this line, however, was a multimillion dollar staff training programme to understand what that line meant. FIRST was actually an acronym for the core values of the bank: Friendly, Informed, Responsive, Service-Oriented and Trustworthy. The acronym translated into how employees were measured and rewarded, it drove the metrics for branch performance, it was the mantra for management and formed the core of the customer feedback system.

Everything was based on measuring staff and management on their ability to be Friendly, Informed, Responsive, Service-Oriented and Trustworthy. Simple, effective, memorable and building a culture.

That's what banks need to focus upon: building strong bank cultures that live the brand.

Forget the adverts. Your people are your adverts.

Banks have no idea how to cross-sell (2008)

An interesting little survey came out this month, looking at the fact that banks do not cross-sell effectively through their call centres. The truth is that most banks do not cross-sell effectively full stop.

I have had the pitch from the teller in the branch who asks me whether I would be interested in a loan or mortgage as I pay in a cheque. To be honest, I would rather walk across broken glass in bare feet than talk to a teller about mortgages.

It is not that I do not like tellers or anything – it is more to do with:

(a) That I am in a rush;

(b) I am only in the branch to do one thing – pay in a cheque; and

(c) I don't want to talk to an administrator about my complex financial dealings.

After all, tellers have been hired, trained and coached to be just transactional administrators haven't they? They certainly have been historically. They have been trained to be box-ticking, button-pushing engines. So how a bank's management team suddenly expects these low-paid transaction engines to transform overnight into super-duper, extrovert, commission-based sales people, is a shocker. A bit like trying to make a pig fly isn't it?

Then we go to the call centre and you find the same thing. I'm ringing the call centre to check a balance, process a request or ask a question. Normally, the call centre person is either efficiently capable of processing my transaction or, for more complex discussions, they refer me back to my branch manager.

"Is there anything else I can help you with sir?"

"Yes, sure. I would like you to hold my hand and explain how 30-year annuity bonds work, in terms of increasing my overall value towards my pension, and whether this is a tax-efficient method of saving for retirement or whether I should look at fund of funds or other savings vehicles."

"Sorry, sir, I didn't quite catch that. Did you say something about your birthday? Happy 30th birthday, sir."

"Actually, I'm after someone who can talk to me about a pension. Is that clear enough?"

"Ah, yessir," says the agent getting excited now as bonus times are ahead, "I can make an appointment for you with our pensions manager on the 30th of never in the branch you only visit to pay cheques into."

Apparently, they cannot deal with me on the telephone because it needs an expert, for regulatory reasons. "Because he's certified", the agent throws in helpfully.

> "What? You mean you have to be legally insane to sell pensions?" I ponder.

> "No sir. He's been certified by the bank to recognise he's had the training to sell, sorry advise you, about pensions, sir."

Ah well, that makes sense, so I go onto the internet and sign into my account.

I've got money sitting in the account just languishing. It's just lying on its back and going, "Look at me, you loser. I'm not earning any interest. I'm not doing anything actually. I'm just sitting in your deposit account and lolling about, you waste of space. Do something with me, won't you?"

Has the bank put an ad in there saying, "Make your balance work harder for you?" Can I see a note anywhere, pointing an arrow at my balance and saying, "We can make sure this earns you cash whilst it's sitting there?" If there is, then it's totally invisible. But then, my internet banking service is just a reflection of the core processing system which administers my account, as in it focuses upon transactions, not sales.

So I finally go into the branch on 30th of never and meet the pensions manager (or is that salesman?).

> "Why did I need to see you", I ask politely. "Why can't we do this over the telephone or internet?"

He's now getting all serious. "For regulatory reasons, I have to see you so that you can fill these forms out in triplicate, sign here and that way I can then say I know you and I've found out all the facts I need to know about you."

> "Blimey", I gulp, "not very twenty-first century is it?"

He then takes me through all of the ins and outs of a pension. After an hour, I've filled in 28 pages of inside leg measurements and mother's maiden names and we shake hands.

"So, there you have it. The stitch-you-up-for-life, never-have-a-spare-penny, hope-you-live-long-enough-to-use-it, made-me-a-nice-earner pension."

"I'll take it", I say.

"OK. We'll get this in the post to you in the next few days, and you then have two weeks to think about it."

"What? Post? Two weeks? I want it now!" I'm always impatient.

"Ah well, by law I have to give you two weeks to think about it, and I have to put it in the post because our bank won't let me email documentation to you." He looks worried now, as he's about to lose a sale.

"OK, I'll think about it. Meantime, do you have anything that can make my money earn interest in my deposit account."

"Oh yes, sir."

So, I walk out of the bank with a brand spanking new deposit account that's been upgraded from no-interest, to low-interest with a free credit card and overdraft facility.

For the bank, they count this as yes, I've been cross-sold two extra products. The deposit account plus a credit card and a loan. After all, by overdraft facility they actually mean loan. So the bank counts me as holding three products: a deposit account, credit card and loan.

The thing is, I see these as all being only one thing – a deposit account. They may count it as three, but I count it as one, and I can close down one product relationship with them very easily.

The true cross-sell, the pension, cannot be sold for regulatory and internal structural reasons. And yet, this is the one product

I wanted to buy, and the one product that would hold me to the bank for life, and probably death.

The real bottom line is that banks have grown up focused upon transactions, payments, money transmissions. Therefore, they sell transaction products. To make them retailers with real sales pizzaz, and advisory high net worth solutions, is darned tough. But there is definitely an opportunity here for banks:

(a) If they want to use branches to cross-sell, then make sure there's someone who is trained to talk to the customer about complex finances inside that branch, or available via a videolink there and then, rather than prompting tellers to embarrassingly ask the question: "would you like a mortgage with that cheque deposit today sir?";

(b) Do the same with the call centre so that if an agent says, "can I help you with anything else" that they can immediately refer the customer to a specialist who is competent in complex finances and not say "oh, we will need to make an appointment for that sort of request sir, can you come into the branch in a fortnight?"; and

(c) Start using internet channels to point out the inefficiencies of my deposits and withdrawals, proactively highlight how I could be more efficient, make automated offers that relate to analysis of my transactions and activities.

Chapter 8 Long-term thinking

The
Complete
Banker

The 'Long Now' of finance, Part 1 (2010)

So I finally got to attend a free lunch! This was the launch of the largest event focused upon using long-term thinking in finance that I've ever seen, and sponsored by many organisations including the Financial Services Club.

Around 400 folks gathered to hear the wise words of legendary thinkers and speakers, including my good friends Professor Michael Mainelli of Z/Yen Group and Bernard Lietaer, along with luminaries Brian Eno (yes, he from Roxy Music), Alexander Rose, Stewart Brand, Professor Sir Roderick Floud and fund manager Edward Bonham Carter. This was all ably chaired by Faisal Islam from Channel 4 News.

The opening session comprised a panel discussing 'The Long Now – Long-Term Thinking and Responsibility in the Framework of the Next 10,000 Years'. What the hell is all that about, you may ask? 10,000 years? Who the hell cares about 10,000 years? Well, a lot of folks do and the Long Now is all about thinking for the long term.

Brian Eno kicked off the session by talking about how the idea came to him, as he is the man everyone pointed to as the creator of the phrase 'the Long Now'. He said the idea came to him when walking around New York and seeing everyone rushing about, real fast. New York – like many capital cities of today – is all about fast. Fast this, fast that. And everyone is passing through, as they don't see New York as their home but as their place of work. So they have very short-term thinking or, as Brian referred to it, they think like a "Short Man".

Ask the Short Man what he's doing, and he'll tell you his plan for today or this week. That's as far as the Short Man thinks. There is no life plan, or after-life plan. Just the Short Now. The issue, however, as anyone thinking about what planet we will be leaving to our children and grandchildren and great grandchildren, is that short-term thinking is killing the planet. So how do we think long term: the Long Now?

It's challenging.

10,000 years from now is 12010 AD (which is why all the material of the Long Now refers to Now years with a 0 precursor; for example, this year is 02010). 10,000 years ago was 7990 BC. There was no civilisation as such then. We had just converted from cavemen to men in caves and beaches and nomadics. Then, around 5000 BC, we became civilised (which is debatable). 10,000 years is hard to imagine or to see as relevant. So what did the Long Now guys do to make it seem more relevant? After all, the aim is to get us to think about what we will be leaving on this planet for the long term, not just today.

The Long Now guys decided to build a clock that would last for 10,000 years. A 10,000 year clock! This would be a physical manifestation of the Long Now to inspire long-term thinking about what we leave on this planet. The Clock was inspired by Danny Hillis, who had just created the world's fastest computer back in the early 1990s, and it is a physical manifestation of the longness of time.

A clock that will last for 10,000 years. The first question is how can you build a clock that will last that long? And Danny responded by creating five guiding principles:

1. **Longevity:** with occasional maintenance, the clock should reasonably be expected to display the correct time for the next 10,000 years;
2. **Maintainability:** the clock should be maintainable with Bronze Age technology;
3. **Transparency:** it should be possible to determine operational principles of the clock by close inspection;
4. **Evolvability:** it should be possible to improve the clock with time;

167

It's Banking Jim, But Not As We Know It

5. **Scalability:** it should be possible to build working models of the clock from table-top to monumental size using the same design.

The five principles can easily apply to anything you want to build for the long term.

The Long Now team then built a prototype of the Clock in 1999, and are now building a massive underground 10,000 year clock in Nevada. The clock has a really impressive algorithm which produces a different order for the ringing of the chimes each and every day for the next 10,000 years. That's over 3.5 million combinations of chimes! Amazing stuff.

All in all, the Long Now is very impressive. It's also very academic, very expensive and very, very, very long-term, which raises the question ... so what? OK, so it's a big underground long now clock, but what's it there for? It's there to get us to think about and answer long-term questions such as, what will happen to the clock if, in 1,000 years, there's another Dark Age? It's to get people to think long term, which is what many are claiming we should now be doing in banking and finance.

And that was the point of this conference. How can we think long? I'll add more to this entry but, for sheer imagination, I like the idea of a 10,000 year clock.

Now, how about an Apple product that stays cool for more than one year?

The Long Now of Finance, Part Two (2010)

How does 10,000 year thinking relate to or work in finance?

The idea is to fund long-term projects. The sort of massive projects that no-one knows how to fund. The sort of project that governments shy away from as politicians only have four-year lives and thinking past the next term in office is hard for them.

The sort of thing like building a pyramid or a cathedral, something that is long lasting and changes humanity forever. Who today would think about building such a thing?

Back in the heady Egyptian and religious fervour days of old, building a huge monolithic testimonial for prayer and worship was the thing to do. But then, back then, you were rewarded with something other than finances.

Today, no-one would build such things. However, there are other things we could, and probably should build, such as flood protection barriers, and the Long Now guys used the example of two countries to illustrate this. One that thinks and funds Long and the other Short.

The Long thinking is in the Netherlands. The Dutch government spent €450 million building the Maeslant barrier to protect the reclaimed land across the coast of the Netherlands.

Rather relying on a boy to stick his finger in the dyke, the Dutch government decided they would fund such a project because, if catastrophe ever struck and the land was flooded, it would pretty much wipe out the most important parts of Holland.

So if you're Dutch, a €450 million spend on an event that may never happen makes sense ... because if it did, the cost could be, let's say, €60 billion. What could cost €60 billion? The devastation and disaster caused by a major flood of the Dutch coast.

And this is also the cost of the sinking of the major American coastal city, New Orleans, in 2005. Hurricane Katrina cost the US over $80 billion. That's €60 billion. If the US had thought long, they would have spent the $1 billion it would have cost to build the flood defences for the southern coastline, and saved themselves $79 billion.

That's the thing about Long Finance, it thinks long-term. It recognises that the investment of millions today will save billions tomorrow. For each euro or dollar spent today, it recognises it will save 100 times that amount tomorrow. So long-term finance thinks long and invests long to save when the short now happens.

Stewart Brand, author of 'Whole Earth Discipline', then expanded on this commentary further by quoting from the classic book by Robert Heinlein. 'Time for the Stars'. In the book, released in 1956, Heinlein recounts the work of the Long Range Foundation (LRF), a foundation that thinks the way outlined above:

> "The charter goes on with a lot of lawyers' fog but the way the directors have interpreted it has been to spend money only on things that no government and no other corporation would touch... To make the LRF directors light up with enthusiasm you had to suggest something that cost a billion or more and probably wouldn't show results for ten generations, if ever ... ."

The key to the LRF is that they only invest in things so expensive and so far out that it wouldn't be investable for a government. However, by adopting this strategy, they have become the most profitable company in the universe, making shedloads of cash thanks to those investments paying off when the inevitable disasters, catastrophes or just plain bets pay off.

The bottom line is that Long Finance and Long Banking looks at uninvestable projects, the big ticket items, and takes them on board precisely because they are good for the long-term health and protection of mankind. That's the nature of the Long Now.

Brian Eno likened it to the story of New College Oxford which, being British, was actually established in 1379 and isn't new at all. The College's Great Hall has this fantastic arched ceiling with oak beams across. After 500 years, the beams inevitably were rotting and decaying so badly they needed to be replaced.

So the Dean of the College asked the groundsmen if they knew of anywhere to source some similar beams? "Oh yes", the head groundsman said. "Five hundred years ago, when they built the college", he told the Dean, "the founders planted a forest of oaks of the same wood as the ones used in the ceiling just over there." In other words, they had had the foresight to realise that, at a point in the Long Future, the ceiling beams would need replacing so they planted trees for just such an occasion in the Long Now.

That's thinking Long, and this is what Long Finance is focusing upon.

I realise all of this sounds a bit tree-hugging or academic, but it's also critically important for those who care about an agenda that focuses upon more the just the right here, right now.

And, just in case you're wondering, yes, the College used the oak trees for their new ceiling and have since planted another small copse of oaks for the next time it may be needed.

The Long Now of Finance, Part Three (2010)

In the last of three reports on the Long Now of Finance, the last part of the day focused upon new ways of banking and supporting 10,000 year thinking, with Bernard Lietaer opening the session with a dialogue around using demurrage to encourage this.

Demurrage is a hard thing to grapple with, as it gets into discussions about fiat currencies and usury which are far beyond the ken of a mere blog on banking ... or it is today anyway. If you want to know the ins and outs of all that stuff then go checkout a book like: "The Creature from Jekyll Island : A Second Look at the Federal Reserve" (ooh, that's fun!), but the gist of the conversation goes something like this.

You plant a tree as an investment in the future. When is it best to chop down the tree, and what is the tree's value in 100 years?

Let's say that you have $100 today, and you can invest that $100 in planting a tree which, in 100 years, will retail at $1,000 based upon today's pricing. So you now think the tree is worth that to you in a hundred years.

No. In 100 years, using interest-based analysis of net present value and assuming you get a positive interest rate of 5% per year, then the tree is worth about $7.60 in 100 years, based upon the deferred costs of your investment. In other words, you are losing 5% per year by having your money tied up in an illiquid asset because you could have been earning 5% interest on that cash by putting it into other more liquid assets with faster, shorter-term returns.

This means you are punished for investing in long-term assets and incentivised to invest in short-term earning vehicles. It is the nature of usury, interest and today's financial market offerings. But it doesn't have to be. According to Bernard, if you use demurrage, you can turn this on its head.

What is demurrage? Normally, it is talking about a fee related to shipping costs but, in this context, it is the carrying cost of money. Here's one definitive view from answers.com:

"Demurrage is a cost associated with owning or holding currency over a given period of time. It is sometimes referred to as a carrying cost of money. For commodity money such as gold, demurrage is in practice nothing more than the cost of storing and securing the gold".

Now it's not a well-known field or term, but it is focused upon making it worthless to keep your cash in short-term things and incentivises to invest in long-term things by exchanging your cash for something else of value, such as a basket of commodities.

So here's Bernard's idea. You take your money and swap it for a Terra. Terra is a complementary currency designed for long-term investing, and 100 Terra = 1 barrel of oil + 10 bushels of wheat + 20 kg of copper + 1/10 oz of gold + 1000 carbon emission units, and so on.

The fact is that here, you are investing in commodities that have lifelong values, so you lose nothing but gain. This is why, when we see a 'flight to safety', it's always oil, gold and commodities that fly through the roof in value. Meanwhile, the storage cost of your basket of commodities is passed to the issuer of the Terra currency who pay a demurrage fee.

The result is that you have a currency exchange that is inflation-proof by definition, automatically convertible without new international treaty, and provides a pure medium of exchange and planning currency, rather than a store of value.

Returning to our tree example therefore, the 100-year old tree is now worth $168,903.82 in 100 years' time, rather than $7.60, based upon the payment of a demurrage fee of 5% per annum.

In other words, it works the opposite way to the usury based system and encourages long-term investing.

It is also complementary to the commercial world of investing, and Bernard totally believes in this proposition. I've known Bernard for over a decade, and he knows his stuff. After all, he's worked and invested alongside George Soros and was formerly a Belgian central banker who came up with the idea of the euro, or the ECU as it was back then.

But ... after a decade, his idea still has not got all the buy-in it should have. This is because people's behaviours won't change unless they have to, and because the thing he's talking about above is darned complex.

That's why fund manager Edward Bonham Carter said: "If you ask people to think about the world in 30 years, they won't because it's not in our nature to do that." Professor Sir Roderick Floud cast doubt on Bernard's contentions too, stating that we over-estimate the extent of market volatility and underestimate the benefits.

The debate raged on, and will do so a long time into the future. The Long Now of the Financial Future, that is.

The learning for me is that there is a way to evolve and morph capitalism for the future to protect us from the crashes of the past and to invest in a sustainable, long-term protection for the planet. However, it's just so complex and difficult that most politicians, regulators, bankers and investors don't understand it, won't invest in it, can't see that far ahead anyway and need a good kicking if anyone wants them to focus upon it, e.g. force them to do it.

I guess that's why Edward Bonham Carter's comment that "there are a lot of clever people out there. The challenge is to get them working on the problems before the dumb people get there", got the biggest laugh of the session.

In their discussion paper, Michael Mainelli and Bob Giffords have laid out a provocative analysis of the global financial crisis in an attempt to widen the debate. The authors have worked hard to raise some new arguments, dismiss some old ones and change the priorities for others. They point out the dangers of an over-zealous regulatory reaction and of trampling over competition in the name of emergency measures, and they argue that a healthy system must be more diverse. Their key point is the importance of competition in open markets to prevent "too big to fail is too big to regulate", and they encourage more radical investigation of Long Finance.